THE
ANASAZI

Other titles in the *Lost Civilizations* series include:

LOST CIVILIZATIONS

THE
ANASAZI

William W. Lace

LUCENT BOOKS

An imprint of Thomson Gale, a part of The Thomson Corporation

Detroit • New York • San Francisco • San Diego • New Haven, Conn. • Waterville, Maine • London • Munich

© 2005 Thomson Gale, a part of The Thomson Corporation.

Thomson and Star Logo are trademarks and Gale and Lucent Books are registered trademarks used herein under license.

For more information, contact
Lucent Books
27500 Drake Rd.
Farmington Hills, MI 48331-3535
Or you can visit our Internet site at http://www.gale.com

LIBRARY OF CONGRESS CATALOGING-IN-PUBLICATION DATA

Lace, William W.
  The Anasazi / by William W. Lace.
    p. cm. — (Lost civilizations)
  Includes bibliographical references and index.
  ISBN 1-59018-563-3 (hardcover : alk. paper)
  1. Pueblo Indians—History. 2. Pueblo Indians—Social life and customs. I. Title. II. Series:
Lost civilizations (San Diego, Calif.)
  E99.P9L32 2005
  978.9'01—dc22

                                                                            2004020000

Printed in the United States of America

CONTENTS

FOREWORD

"What marvel is this?" asked the noted eighteenth-century German poet and philosopher, Friedrich Schiller. "O earth . . . what is your lap sending forth? Is there life in the deeps as well? A race yet unknown hiding under the lava?" The "marvel" that excited Schiller was the discovery, in the early 1700s, of two entire ancient Roman cities buried beneath over sixty feet of hardened volcanic ash and lava near the modern city of Naples, on Italy's western coast. "Ancient Pompeii is found again!" Schiller joyfully exclaimed. "And the city of Hercules rises!"

People had known about the existence of long-lost civilizations before Schiller's day, of course. Stonehenge, a circle of huge, very ancient stones had stood, silent and mysterious, on a plain in Britain as long as people could remember. And the ruins of temples and other structures erected by the ancient inhabitants of Egypt, Palestine, Greece, and Rome had for untold centuries sprawled in magnificent profusion throughout the Mediterranean world. But when, why, and how were these monuments built? And what were the exact histories and beliefs of the peoples who built them? A few scattered surviving ancient literary texts had provided some partial answers to some of these questions. But not until Pompeii and Herculaneum started to emerge from the ashes did the modern world begin to study and re-

construct lost civilizations in a systematic manner.

Even then, the process was at first slow and uncertain. Pompeii, a bustling, prosperous town of some twenty thousand inhabitants, and the smaller Herculaneum met their doom on August 24, A.D. 79, when the nearby volcano, Mt. Vesuvius, blew its top and literally erased them from the map. For nearly seventeen centuries, their contents, preserved in a massive cocoon of volcanic debris, rested undisturbed. Not until the early eighteenth century did people begin raising statues and other artifacts from the buried cities; and at first this was done in a haphazard, unscientific manner. The diggers, who were seeking art treasures to adorn their gardens and mansions, gave no thought to the historical value of the finds. The sad fact was that at the time no trained experts existed to dig up and study lost civilizations in a proper manner.

This unfortunate situation began to change in 1763. In that year, Johann J. Winckelmann, a German librarian fascinated by antiquities (the name then used for ancient artifacts), began to investigate Pompeii and Herculaneum. Although he made some mistakes and drew some wrong conclusions, Winckelmann laid the initial, crucial groundwork for a new science—archaeology (a term derived from two Greek words meaning "to talk about ancient things").

His book, *History of the Art of Antiquity*, became a model for the first generation of archaeologists to follow in their efforts to understand other lost civilizations. "With unerring sensitivity," noted scholar C.W. Ceram explains, "Winckelmann groped toward original insights, and expressed them with such power of language that the cultured European world was carried away by a wave of enthusiasm for the antique ideal. This . . . was of prime importance in shaping the course of archaeology in the following century. It demonstrated means of understanding ancient cultures through their artifacts."

In the two centuries that followed, archaeologists, historians, and other scholars began to piece together the remains of lost civilizations around the world. The glory that was Greece, the grandeur that was Rome, the cradles of human civilization in Egypt's Nile valley and Mesopotamia's Tigris-Euphrates valley, the colorful royal court of ancient China's Han Dynasty, the mysterious stone cities of the Maya and Aztecs in Central America—all of these

and many more were revealed in fascinating, often startling, if sometimes incomplete, detail by the romantic adventure of archaeological research. This work, which continues, is vital. "Digs are in progress all over the world," says Ceram. "For we need to understand the past five thousand years in order to master the next hundred years."

Each volume in the Lost Civilizations series examines the history, works, everyday life, and importance of ancient cultures. The archaeological discoveries and methods used to gather this knowledge are stressed throughout. Where possible, quotes by the ancients themselves, and also by later historians, archaeologists, and other experts support and enliven the text. Primary and secondary sources are carefully documented by footnotes and each volume supplies the reader with an extensive Works Consulted list. These and other research tools afford the reader a thorough understanding of how a civilization that was long lost has once more seen the light of day and begun to reveal its secrets to its captivated modern descendants.

EMPTY GRANDEUR

Wind and snow swirling about them, Richard Wetherill and Charlie Mason rode through the juniper forest high atop Mesa Verde in southwestern Colorado looking for stray cattle. They found instead, on that raw December day in 1888, the empty ruins of a vanished civilization.

Coming to the edge of a canyon, they peered through the white mist, glimpsing what Wetherill later called "a magnificent city"[1] nestled under the overhang of the opposite cliff. They quickly abandoned the search for their cattle and rode around the canyon rim to a spot from which they could descend, using handholds that—although they could not have known it—had been hacked out of the sandstone some seven hundred years earlier.

The two men reached a long, deep shelf and spent the remaining daylight hours exploring what Wetherill named Cliff Palace. They gazed up at stone towers four stories high, clambered over walls, squeezed through windows, and wandered through room after room. In many, they found pottery and tools stacked as if their owners would momentarily return.

Something else Wetherill and Mason could not have known was that what they saw at Cliff Palace—and about 90 percent of what visitors see today—was almost exactly as it was seven hundred years ago, with little restoration and reinforcement by the National Park Service needed. Thomas E. Mails, an expert on Pueblo architecture, writes, "Inevitably, one asks how they did it. And even when some of the answers have been learned, amazement remains. Nowhere in North America is there a feat of ancient architecture to rival that of the cliff dwellings, built without the aid of nails, bolts, trusses, or any tool of consequence."[2]

The questions occurring to Wetherill and Mason doubtless were the same asked by Spanish explorers and American frontiersmen who had seen similar ruins throughout what today is called the Four Corners—the area in which Colorado, New Mexico, Arizona, and Utah meet. Who built these marvels of engineering and when? Why did they leave? Where did they go?

The Navajo Answer
The logical place to ask was among those living nearby, principally the Navajo Indians who often acted as guides. The abandoned cities, the Navajo said, had been built by the *anaa'i bi zazi*, or Anasazi, which has been translated as "ancestors of our enemies" or, more politely, "ancestors of people not like us."

Today, a paved highway leads to Mesa Verde and a gently winding trail leads down to Cliff Palace. The rooms in which the Anasazi lived and the round kivas in which they worshipped are now home only to birds, mice, lizards, and the occasional wandering mountain lion. The same questions, however, continue to confront the thousands of tourists who flock there and to other similar sites in the region.

Most of these questions have been answered at least somewhat satisfactorily. Archaeologists have discovered much about how the Anasazi developed and lived. Technology has allowed scholars to pinpoint both when the cities were built and when they were abandoned.

There is even general agreement on what happened to the inhabitants. Far from vanishing, they likely migrated east to become the Pueblo Indian tribes along the Rio Grande in New Mexico; south to become the Zuni, Laguna, and Acoma; and west to become the Hopi.

"No Mystery"

Some of the descendants of the Anasazi—who much prefer terms such as the Hopi "hisatsinom," or "our ancestors"—have a different perspective. "Those places are still

Cliff Palace glows in the afternoon sun at Mesa Verde, Colorado. Swedish archaeologist Gustaf Nordenskiöld, who explored Cliff Palace in the 1890s, likened the ancient city to an enchanted castle.

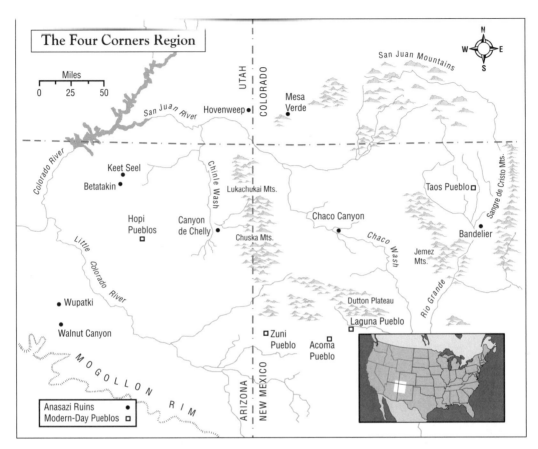

The Four Corners Region

Anasazi Ruins •
Modern-Day Pueblos □

alive with the spirits of my forebears," writes Christine Suina of the Cochiti tribe. "It's no mystery to us! We may have moved a few hundreds of miles away but we are very much still a part of those who survived and lived in Mesa Verde and other places now in ruins."[3]

The Anasazi can be likened to the century plant, a type of cactus that is a feature of the southwestern landscape. The century plant lives about twenty-five years, not one hundred, and blooms only at the end of its life when the spike of yellow flowers grows so fast that the plant dies, having expended all its energy. In much the same way, the Anasazi culture developed slowly over the centuries. Its flowering came between A.D.

1050 and 1300 in the so-called Classic Pueblo period. Like the century plant, however, this flowering was brief, and the blooms—the magnificent great houses of Cliff Palace, Pueblo Bonito, Betatakin, and all the rest—would shortly be abandoned and fall into ruin.

There is no lack of theories as to why this great civilization withered. Drought, say some scientists. Hostile enemies, say others. Changes in religion, still others claim. The theories, however, remain just that. When all the evidence is examined, the mystery of the Anasazi is, in the words of University of Colorado professor Linda Cordell, "an open book."[4]

CHAPTER ONE

THE
ANCIENT ONES

Scientists disagree as to when or from where the ancestors of the Anasazi arrived in the Americas. The descendants of the Anasazi have versions all their own. All agree, however, that long before the fabulous cities were built, the forebears of those who built them roamed the Four Corners.

The most prevalent theory as to the origin of those variously called Native Americans, American Indians, or Amerinds is that they migrated in waves across the Bering Strait at times when there was a land bridge between Russian Siberia and Alaska and then spread throughout North and South America. Present-day Indians and the people of eastern Asia share many common physical characteristics. In addition, scientists have found similarities in DNA—the basic genetic building block—between Indians and the people of Siberia.

If the Anasazi's ancestors did, indeed, cross from Asia on a land bridge as many as thirty thousand years ago, that bridge had been created by the most recent Ice Age, during which immense glaciers spread south from the North Pole. Forming these glaciers required huge amounts of ocean water. As a result, ocean levels were much lower, turning what is now a string of islands in the Bering Strait into solid land.

Other research, however, points in another direction—westward across the Pacific Ocean. Traces of DNA found in some ancient Indian remains in South America contain a mutation that, while not found in Siberia, is common in South China and Polynesia.

Since this genetic mutation has not been found in Indian remains to the north, the question is, how did it show up to the south if all Indian ancestors migrated from Siberia? Conjecture—and it remains just that in the absence of physical evidence—is that there was a migration by boat or canoe from the South Pacific.

The Clovis Points

Scientists question not only from where Indians came, but also when. Although the land bridge likely existed some thirty thousand years ago, no evidence proved that humans lived in the Americas earlier than about 10,000 B.C. This estimate was based on the discovery of spear points found near Clovis, New Mexico, among the bones of an extinct mammal shown by radiocarbon dating to have been killed about that time.

More recent research, however, has yielded different results. Linguists comparing speech patterns between modern Siberian

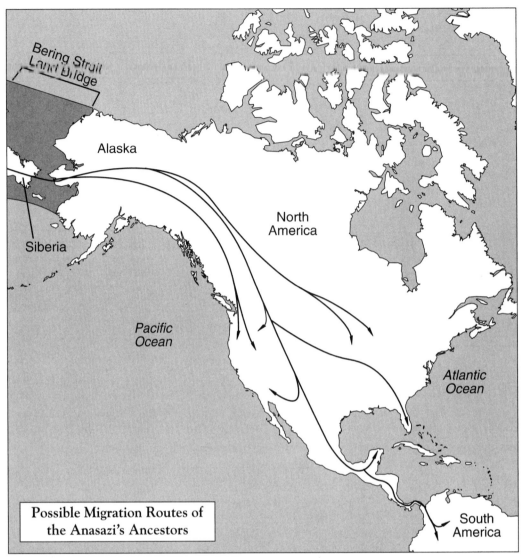

**Possible Migration Routes of
the Anasazi's Ancestors**

peoples and American Indians say the migration could have been anytime from 10,000 to 33,000 B.C. Comparisons of the DNA of ancient Indian bones with those of their supposed relatives in Siberia show a difference that yields a date of 38,000 B.C. Therefore, as anthropologist Theodore G. Schurr of the University of Pennsylvania writes, "There is, indeed, little agreement and much confusion."[5]

Yet there is little confusion among many of the modern descendants of the Anasazi

as to their ancestral roots. According to legend, their people have inhabited the Four Corners forever, or at least since the first humans emerged from the underworld onto the face of the earth through the *sipapu*, or point of origin.

The Pueblo tribes may differ on the exact location of the *sipapu* or in details of the underworld or underworlds, but these all are variations on the same theme. These accounts of the creation are remarkably similar and are powerful arguments for a common ancestry.

Whether one embraces the scientific or traditional view, however, all agree that humans have lived in the Four Corners for a very long time—at least since 10,000 B.C.

Scientists disagree as to whether these Paleo-Indians, or "ancient" Indians, as those who lived in the Four Corners at the time the Clovis points were created have been termed, were the forebears of the Anasazi. There is no direct evidence that they were—no undisputable links from distant to more recent past. Some experts, citing similarities between later developments and those in other parts of the Southwest, claim the Anasazi migrated to their eventual homeland from present-day Nevada. Again, however, no direct link has been found. So, as with much else about the Anasazi, their heritage remains in question.

People on the Move

Science has shown that Four Corners in 10,000 B.C. was a far different place than at present. The Ice Age was ending and glaciers were in a slow retreat, but the climate of the Four Corners was still cold and wet—

THE ZUNI VIEW OF CREATION

While scientists may debate over how and when human beings first came to the Americas, American Indians have their own versions that have been handed down, first orally and only much later in writing, over thousands of years. At a conference in 1990 dealing with the Anasazi, Edmund Ladd, a member of the Zuni tribe, gave his people's version, found in *The Anasazi: Why Did They Leave? Where Did They Go?* edited by Jerold G. Widdison:

In the very beginning, the very beginning of time, there were no humans in the world. Sun Father came up in the east, he came up and went over the mountains, over the sea, rested at high noon for a spell, and descended to the west and went into the western ocean, and night fell. All night long, all night long Sun Father traveled under the earth, and he traveled until he came to the east again to bring a new day. But the new day was not filled with joy, the new day was not filled with laughter. All he could hear was cries of his children in Mother Earth's womb. So he created these twin war gods, the Twin Gods. And he said unto them, "Go and bring my children up in my light." And so they did. But the origin was one that was many faceted. They moved up from the lower earth below, and they started moving. They moved every four years, and in all directions.

much more so than it is today. The plains, now desert, were covered with grasses, vegetation that supported a variety of large animals—mammoths, bison, giant elk. It was in these surroundings that the Paleo-Indians lived, hunting the animals and gathering edible plants.

Since the animals were constantly on the move, the people moved with them. They probably constructed primitive, temporary shelters from skins, branches, and twigs, although no traces remain in the Four Corners. Remains of such shelters from the Paleo-Indian time period have been found in Chile, however, so scientists speculate that people elsewhere built them as well.

The hunters did not yet have bows and arrows. They faced their prey armed with spears and with the atlatl, a stick used to propel small spears or darts that were placed in a grooved slot. The atlatl served as an extension of the arm, making it possible for hunters to hurl darts greater distances and with more accuracy than they could by hand.

The spear and dart points were laboriously fashioned by striking flakes from pieces of flint until they achieved the desired shape—flat and tapered to a point. The edges were sharpened to a keen edge except at the rear, where they were bound with leather thongs to the dart or spear shaft.

These points varied in size according to the size of game. Designs of these points also varied from one location and time period to another. So distinctive are these designs that scientists have named the points according to where they have been found—Clovis being the earliest—and have been able to track movements of different Paleo-Indian bands.

Since their prey was large and their weapons small, hunters often had to make good use of the terrain in order to achieve some of their kills. Bones found on canyon floors at the base of cliffs indicate that animals were trapped by the hunters. In some cases, the collection of bones is huge, signifying that a herd of animals might have been stampeded off the cliffs to their deaths.

Warmer Weather

Game, however, was not always plentiful nor hunting successful. As the Ice Age waned, the herds of larger animals migrated back to the North. The climate slowly warmed and became drier, and vegetation for grazing was in shorter supply.

With most of the game gone, the land could not support a large human population, and scientists have estimated that the number of people in the Four Corners varied only between about 2,000 and 6,000, averaging 1 person to every forty square miles. (By comparison, the most sparsely populated country on earth today, Mongolia, has 4.3 persons for every one square mile.)

This sparseness of population meant that family or clan groups interacted only infrequently, thus limiting the spread of innovation, such as improved weapons. In addition, changes to the natural environment were almost imperceptible, giving the people little reason to innovate. For about five thousand years, there was virtually no change in the Paleo-Indians' way of life. A new type of stone knife might show up every millennium, but each generation lived pretty much exactly as those before. "Doing things precisely as one's forebears had was a formula for success," writes University of New

Hunting with an Atlatl

An atlatl is a carved wooden hunting device used for launching a flexible spear at high speeds. In effect, it lengthens the hunter's arm and enables him to throw a spear much farther and with more force than he could without it.

Spear

Atlatl

The hunter positions the spear in the atlatl and aims at his prey.

Under acceleration by the atlatl, the dart flexes and compresses like a spring, storing energy to be used to push itself away from the atlatl and launching at speeds that easily exceed 100 miles an hour. A spear thrown with an atlatl can kill a deer at 40 yards and will fly more than 200 yards.

Mexico anthropologist David E. Stuart. "Their forebears had survived, and survival meant success."[6]

Hunters and gatherers can and do alter their ways of life if faced with dramatic environmental change, and such a change began about 5000 B.C. The gradual warming trend accelerated. By 4000 B.C. Four Cor-

ners had entered an era known to climatologists as the Altithermal, in which climatic conditions were harsher even than those of today. Annual rainfall, now eight to ten inches a year, was only four to six inches. The peak temperature in summer was about 112°F, whereas today it rarely exceeds 105°F.

Smaller Game

As the Altithermal took hold, the remaining herds of large animals moved north, their places taken by rabbits, rodents, and smaller variety of deer. There was insufficient game to enable the Paleo-Indians to maintain their traditional diet consisting principally of meat supplemented by wild plants.

Some groups followed the large animals, unwilling to adapt to new conditions. Others stayed behind and found new ways to survive. Perhaps newcomers from other areas of the Southwest brought new technology with them. There is no way to know for certain.

What is known from the remains of campsites is that life was very different in Four Corners during and after the Altithermal. With meat scarce, people had to diversify their diet by eating more plants. They did not yet have agriculture—that is, they had not reached the point of planting and harvesting crops. They did, however, put to use the knowledge of local plants gained over thousands of years.

In all likelihood, they had previously thought some of these plants inedible or not worth the trouble of making edible. It was too easy to pick berries or nuts. Now, necessity drove them to add new plants to their

LONGER LIVES LONGER AGO

Life expectancy is generally thought to increase with the passing of centuries. Because of better medical care, more nutritious diets, and the ability to take vitamin supplements, people today live longer on average than did their ancestors. It would seem, then, that the Paleo-Indian and Archaic peoples would have had shorter life spans than the Anasazi who came after them. In his book *A.D. 1250*, Lawrence W. Cheek says this is not necessarily so:

Common-sense archaeology assumed that Paleo-Indian and Archaic lives were short and hard, but common sense may be wrong. As long as game was plentiful, hunter-gatherers spent less time making their living—getting the food they needed to survive—than agriculturists. Their diet was more varied and richer in protein, and because they only counted on native plants and animals, they didn't have to worry about crop failure in dry years. The lives of the prehistoric Southwestern farmers, who would appear thousands of years later, were vastly more complicated and tenuous. Some anthropologists think humans took up farming as a last resort, only after their population had overwhelmed the truly natural resources.

diet and to find new ways of cooking them. One example was the yucca, whose tough root is high in food value, especially starch, but which had to be boiled.

Boiling yucca roots was a laborious process, since pottery had not yet made its way to the Four Corners. Instead, campsites from this period feature cooking pits that were probably lined with either animal skins or clay. Yucca roots were cooked in these pits, the water having been boiled by dropping in stones that had been heated over coals. The process must have been tedious, requiring many trips between the fires and cooking pits. Large numbers of stones, reddened by fire and cracked by contact with cold water, have been found at such campsites.

New Tools

Scientists have also found, along with evidence of cooking techniques, a new variety of tools. Paleo-Indian tools had been mostly those associated with hunting—spear and dart points, hide scrapers, knives, and awls. The change to a more vegetarian diet brought about much greater use of grinding stones, choppers, and scrapers designed for stripping seeds from grain stalks. Scientists named these newer tools "archaic," and the same term is used to label the entire period from 5000 B.C. to A.D. 1.

Some people who remained in Four Corners during the Altithermal probably resisted change and tried to retain the hunter lifestyle. These groups, their food supply restricted, would likely have produced fewer children, limiting reproduction either through abortions or restriction of sexual activity. Eventually they disappeared or were absorbed by others. As Stuart

The Anasazi used the root of the yucca for food and the plant's fibers to make clothing.

writes, "Those more willing to experiment, or more desperate, fared better, so their behavior eventually became traditional among their more numerous descendants. . . . This was the Southwest's first great lesson on the merits of progress."[7]

Those Indians who depended more on gathering than hunting not only survived during the Altithermal, but also thrived—or at least increased in population. As Stuart on plains, the Archaic Indians' largely vegetarian diet, while it lacked much of the fat and protein of meat, was actually higher in calories. The people were healthier and tended to have greater numbers of children than the Paleo-Indians who clung to the old ways.

This increase in population is reflected in the size of successive Archaic campsites. These camps were in locations much like those at which the Anasazi would later build their cities—at higher elevations, near the heads of canyons, and just below the canyon rims. Water was more plentiful here than in the lower desert, coming not from rivers or streams but from seeps—groundwater trickling out through the canyon wall. And where water was more plentiful, so was edible vegetation.

A Pattern Emerges

The people of the Archaic period not only occupied camps larger than those of the Paleo-Indians but also returned to them again and again over many years. The cooking pits and fire pits show evidence of constant reuse. It is the first indication in the Four Corners of movement toward a more settled way of life.

There are even signs of early experimentation with agriculture. Near some of the sites are clumps of wild yucca, growing at elevations far higher than where they normally grow. Some scientists speculate that the yucca might have been deliberately transplanted from where they naturally grew.

By 3000 B.C. the climatic pendulum had swung the other way. The hot, dry conditions of the Altithermal abated, and the Four Corners became cooler and wetter,

though nowhere to the extent as in the millennia after the Ice Age. Grassy plains covered what had been desert, and some of the larger animals returned.

About the same time, an improved type of dart point—known today as the San Jose—came to Four Corners. Like its predecessors, it was sharp along the leading edges but was triangular and barbed in the way usually associated with arrowheads. This point would strike deep into the hunted animal, with the barbs preventing it from being dislodged. Even if the dart failed to kill the animal outright, the San Jose points created wounds that bled profusely, making it possible for the hunter to track the stricken prey.

The combination of plentiful game and more advanced gathering and cooking techniques made possible a sizable growth in population. Estimates are that by about 2500 B.C. the population had increased from the two thousand to six thousand of the Paleo-Indian period to between fifteen thousand and thirty thousand in the Archaic.

Lessons Learned

After 2500 B.C. the near-ideal conditions of the San Jose period gave way to a climate much like that of the present. The Altithermal, however, had taught the Indians the value of diversity, adaptation, and innovation. Campsites from the later Archaic period, for instance, have yielded many more specialized tools such as those used for grinding acorns and the tasty nuts of the piñon pine tree.

The grinding technique was one used throughout the Americas and is still used by the descendants of the Anasazi. The material to be ground was placed in depressions

These shallow depressions in a sandstone boulder in Utah were used for grinding corn to make flour. Anasazi women placed corn kernels in the depressions and ground them with a handheld rock.

hollowed out of boulders, then ground with a handheld stone, or mano. Later, portable grinding troughs, or metates, were developed.

Yet, as the climate grew warmer, even these relatively sophisticated technological innovations failed to produce enough food for the growing population. The Indians of the Four Corners had learned much over ten thousand years, yet might well have suffered widespread starvation or been forced to shrink their population by having fewer children. Instead, yet another innovation appeared—agriculture—and it would mark the beginning of a series of developments that would lead directly to the Anasazi.

Dendrochronology

Visitors to the ruins of Anasazi buildings will notice—if they look very closely—what appear to be tiny brass circles on some of the wooden roof beams and poles. If they look even closer, they may be able to make out a series of numbers on each circle.

These circles mark spots where core samples have been taken from the wood to determine its age. This is done through a science known as dendrochronology, developed in the 1920s by Andrew E. Douglas.

Douglas discovered that each of the concentric rings within the trunks of certain trees represents a year's growth. Furthermore, he showed that the width of each ring varied according to the climate and rainfall of a given year.

By matching the rings on a living tree with those of trees previously cut and finding points of overlap, it has been possible to tell by looking at tree rings of an ancient trunk or branch exactly when it was cut.

The process is currently highly accurate in dating roof beams and other wooden building materials as far back as 53 B.C.

Although dendrochronology is so accurate that scientists can sometimes tell in what month a tree was cut, it has drawbacks. It cannot distinguish, for instance, between when a tree was cut and when it was first used, and thus can be confusing in cases where a tree trunk was reused.

Radiocarbon Dating

While dendrochronology, or tree-ring dating, is the most widely used by archaeologists in the American Southwest, it cannot pinpoint the age of tree trunks and other wooden building materials beyond about two thousand years. In order to fix the dates of more ancient remains and artifacts, scientists frequently turn to the radiocarbon or C-14 method.

In 1947, American chemist Willard Libby discovered that a small quantity of carbon 14, an isotope, or variation of a chemical element, is present in every living plant and animal. When the organism dies, the C-14 begins a slow process of decay.

Libby developed a method of measuring the amount of decay that had taken place. This has made it possible for scientists to take material, such as bone, leather, or twigs, from a once-living plant or animal as old as fifty thousand years and determine with reasonable accuracy when the organism died.

Libby's discovery won him the Nobel Prize for chemistry, and anthropologist Desmond Clark, quoted on www.c-14dating.com, said that without C-14 dating, "we would still be foundering in a sea of imprecisions sometimes bred of inspired guesswork but more often of imaginative speculation."[8]

CHAPTER TWO

THE BASKETMAKERS

Like a ball rolling downhill, technological or social change picks up speed over time. Certainly this was true with the Indians of the American Southwest. The five hundred to seven hundred years after the Archaic period saw more advancement in civilization than the preceding ten thousand. In the Four Corners, people first identifiable as Anasazi appeared. Known as the Basketmakers, they moved from a nomadic to a settled way of life, thus paving the way for the great developments to follow.

Scientists prefer not to be specific about when the Basketmaker period began. It was

This well-preserved Anasazi basket features a bird design. The Anasazi made such baskets by winding willow or yucca fibers into a tight spiral.

well under way by 100 B.C., but for how long is uncertain. Most classification schemes, therefore, begin with Basketmaker II. No definite proof of a Basketmaker I era has been found, and science—for now—is content to say that the earliest Basketmakers were indistinguishable from the latest Archaic people.

The era took its name from yet another discovery by Richard Wetherill. Excavating Anasazi ruins in Utah in the 1880s, he found, at a level beneath burials of the usual type, bodies from what was clearly an earlier time. Unlike Anasazi graves, these contained no pottery. Instead, large baskets had been placed over the heads of the graves' occupants. Wetherill termed these people "Basketmakers," and the name stuck.

Depite the name, it was not the Basketmakers' weaving ability that set them apart from other people of the Archaic period. Rather, it was their introduction of and gradual dependence on agriculture for the production of food.

The Importance of Corn

Corn was the staple food for the Anasazi and has continued to be so for descendants to the present day. The Anasazi would come to depend so completely on corn that the cycle of planting and harvest and need for rain became the focus of their religion and involved almost every aspect of their daily lives.

Corn is thought to have been developed in Mexico or Central America about 3000 B.C. by the crossing, either deliberately or accidentally, of different strains of grasses. Scientists disagree as to when and how corn reached the Anasazi, though all think it unlikely that the grain was independently de-

veloped by them. What scientists do know is that other early peoples to the south, the Mogollon and Hohokam, were cultivating corn long before any traces appear among the Basketmakers. Estimates of when corn was first grown in the Four Corners vary from 1500 B.C. to A.D. 1.

This earliest corn, whenever it arrived, bore little resemblance to its modern cousins. It was a small-cobbed brown variety of popcorn known as *chapalote* that was ground to make flour. It was not as high in nutritional value as later varieties but was an important supplement to the diet of the early Basketmakers.

Another vegetable, squash, arrived in the Four Corners about the same time as corn. However, given the large number of varieties of squash, researchers think they probably came from multiple sources. Squash and corn were planted together, the leaves on the low-growing vines providing a protective ground cover for the cornstalks.

The Addition of Beans

About A.D. 500 the third major vegetable group, beans, made its appearance. They were added to the planting mix, their tendrils growing up and around the cornstalks. These beans, like the corn, came by way of Mexico. Related to the modern pinto bean, they contained high amounts of lysine, an amino acid essential for body growth that is also found in meat, although not in the same quantity.

The introduction of agriculture did not immediately lead to a settled or sedentary lifestyle. In fact, University of Oklahoma anthropologist Paul Minnis called this development "a monumental non-event."[9] Climatic conditions were such that game, wild grains,

These dried corncobs were found in a cave in Arizona's Superstition Mountains. The earliest form of corn in the American Southwest was a small-cobbed variety known as chapalote.

and other naturally occurring foods still provided the bulk of Basketmaker diets. The Basketmakers did not live near their crops but instead remained at the sites only long enough to plant, tend, and harvest. The rest of the time was spent roaming the area much as had their Archaic forebears.

Hunting, in fact, became more efficient during the Basketmaker II period with the introduction, sometime around A.D. 450, of the bow and arrow. The first Anasazi bows were made of a single piece of hardwood, about three feet long, and had a pull of about fifty pounds, far less powerful than those used at the same time by the tribes on the Great Plains to the north. They were, however, a vast improvement over the atlatl, whose effective range was only about forty yards. Even so, the atlatl would continue to see some use for several centuries.

The Basketmakers farmed, for the most part, in the sandy soil on canyon floors, living in campsites just below the rims. They lived in shelters much like those inhabited by their ancestors. When temperatures grew cooler each fall, they set up campsites in caves. These were not deep, dark holes in the ground, but shallow recesses created

WHAT'S IN A NAME?

The term *Anasazi* referring to the ancient people of Four Corners is one that pleases or satisfies practically nobody. It was introduced into science by cowboy-archaeologist Richard Wetherill after he asked his Navajo guides who had lived in these magnificent buildings they showed him. They answered *anaa'i bi zazi*, most often translated "ancestors of our enemies."

Present-day Pueblo Indians, widely believed to be the descendants of the Anasazi, dislike the term because it is a Navajo word, and the Navajo and Pueblo have, indeed, been enemies at various times. *Pueblo* is a bit more palatable, but is still a foreign word. The first Spanish explorers, seeing the Indian villages of the Southwest, called them *pueblo*—the Spanish word for town. There is not a single Indian word, however, that encompasses all the Pueblo people. Instead, each tribe has its own name for itself—the *Hopitu-Shimunu* for the Hopi or the *Ashiwi* for the Zuni.

Anasazi also does not find much favor among the Navajo, who reject the notion that their ancestors came to Four Corners after the Anasazi had left. They claim to have been in the region long beforehand and, like the Pueblo, to be descended from the Anasazi. Some writers and scientists have tried to come up with a substitute. "Ancestral Puebloan" crops up often, but as archaeologist Linda Cordell writes in *Prehistory of the Southwest*, "Archaeologists are themselves tradition-bound and would not be dissuaded from continuing to use the term Anasazi."

where sections of sandstone had eroded from under the canyon rim. Well-lighted and airy, they could range from a few square feet to hundreds of square yards and offered protection from the elements.

The Need for Storage

As more bounteous crops were harvested, places for storing them were needed. Corn and beans, especially, could be dried and set aside for use during the bitter winter months when nothing could grow. Rather than take all their food supplies with them on their travels, the Basketmakers dug storage pits in the caves. The availability of stored food gave them the flexibility to adapt to variations in climate.

Domesticated plants such as corn led to other advances in technology. As dependence on corn increased, more had to be ground. The old metates gave way to larger versions and manos wielded with two hands instead of one in a back-and-forth rather than circular motion.

The other major development was the advent of pottery, which was far superior to baskets for food storage as well as being a major step forward in cooking. Now, food could be boiled directly over a fire in pots rather than using heated stones. Pottery also added beans to the diet, since there was now a way to cook them—impossible to accomplish in cooking pits.

Pottery first appeared among the Basketmakers about A.D. 300 to 400. They probably learned about it from the Mogollon to the south. Whether they adopted the Mogollon technique of firing clay objects or developed their own by trial and error is not known.

However they were made, Basketmaker II pots were strictly utilitarian—a uniform, dull gray with no attempt at decoration. Varied shapes, colors, and decorations would only appear toward the end of the Basketmaker period.

The storage pits also meant that groups were more likely to return to the same campsite each winter. Refuse, such as cloth fragments, found in some of the pits indicates they might even have been slept in during the coldest weather. From this, it was only a short jump to the construction of underground dwellings known as pithouses.

The large clay pot in this photo, known as an olla, was used to store water, while the three smaller pots were most likely used as cooking vessels.

The First Pithouses

The earliest pithouses were small, large enough for only one family. The builders first used sticks and flat stones to scoop out a round or oval pit anywhere from ten to twenty-five feet across. The pit was dug as deep as possible to take maximum advantage of the ground's insulating properties. Five feet was optimum—anything deeper was unnecessary because of the short stature of the people—but the texture of the soil, especially in caves, sometimes limited depth to little more than three feet.

Since even the firmest soil tended to crumble eventually, the Basketmakers lined the walls with stone slabs or plastered them with clay. The floor was hard-packed dirt with a stone or clay-lined fire pit in the center. In later Basketmaker pithouses, small tunnels were dug at floor level, extending horizontally then turning upward to the surface to act as ventilation shafts. Frequently, an upright stone slab would be placed a few feet in front of the ventilator opening to protect the fire pit from the incoming draft.

The aboveground portion of the pithouse was constructed of wood, another reason for digging the pit as deep as possible, since wood was scarce and harder to work with. Four vertical poles, their tops extending aboveground, were arranged in a square and connected with horizontal beams to form the main roof support. Smaller poles were laid across the support for framing, and similar poles were slanted from the edge of the roof to the ground to complete the walls. The walls and roof were covered with twigs and branches and then plastered with a layer of mud, the only opening a hole in the center of the roof that acted as both an entrance and a smoke vent.

Sporadic Settlement

Scientists long considered the earliest clusters of pithouses—dated about A.D. 200 to 400—as the first permanent settlements. Analysis of trash heaps beside them, however, indicate that they were lived in only a few months a year. At other times the Basketmakers continued their seminomadic ways.

The advent of agriculture provided the margin between starvation and survival during several centuries in which the climate for agriculture was terrible at the worst, inconsistent at the best. Famine might well have forced the Basketmakers to limit their population and remain hunter-gatherers. In such a case, the technological advances of the period would have been unrealized or at least delayed. As it was, however, the people of Basketmaker II, while they did not exactly prosper, were nevertheless poised to take advantage of an opportunity for prosperity.

That opportunity arrived about A.D. 500, when rainfall and temperature became stable and remained so for several centuries. Conditions were good for agriculture, and new plants made farming even more productive for society. By A.D. 700 the Basketmaker Anasazi had made the transition to a settled, farming-based way of life.

Giving up the traditional lifestyle could not have been easy, and the transition to more settled ways was probably very slow. The pace of change had always been very slow in the Four Corners, with people reluctant to abandon proven methods of surviving, as evidenced by the continued use of the atlatl even after the introduction of the bow and arrow. Moreover, farming was hard, tedious work, far different from the

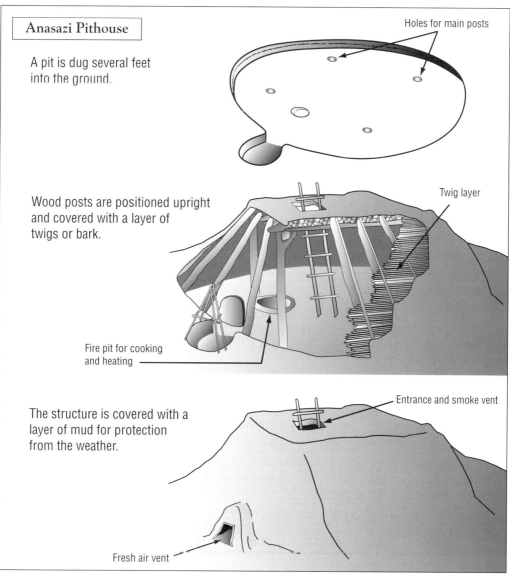

Anasazi Pithouse

A pit is dug several feet into the ground.

Holes for main posts

Wood posts are positioned upright and covered with a layer of twigs or bark.

Twig layer

Fire pit for cooking and heating

The structure is covered with a layer of mud for protection from the weather.

Entrance and smoke vent

Fresh air vent

excitement of the hunt. As anthropologist Charles Avery Amsden wrote, a farmer's success "lies in slow, patient application to the routine of toil of gaining a living, year after year, from one small plot of ground. He dare not wander far . . . his world, visible and invisible, bears a very different aspect."[10]

Indeed, not every group of Basketmakers made the break with the ancient way of life. Archaeological evidence shows that some groups used agriculture only as a supplement to their food supply, relying chiefly on game and wild plants. They tended to have fewer children than the farmers, who welcomed every pair of hands able to work.

THE MODIFIED BASKETMAKERS

The Basketmaker III people who made the important step from hunting and gathering to more of a dependence on agriculture have sometimes been called the Modified Basketmakers because of the changes in their lifestyles. Scientists have speculated that much of the change they instituted was as a result of contact with other southwestern peoples, such as the Mogollon and Hohokam.

In his book *Anasazi: Ancient People of the Rock*, Donald G. Pike says that, no matter where the ideas for change came from, they were to lead to an era of almost unparalleled development:

> Exactly where the plateau people picked up their new tricks cannot be known with any degree of certainty. It is apparent that they were an easygoing, gregarious folk who got on well with their neighbors and most strangers, a condition of personality that made trade with other regions of the Southwest a natural endeavor. Because of this trade, and some striking similarities of artifacts, it is most easily assumed that the Basketmakers learned much of what they did from the Mogollon and Hohokam. . . . Whatever the impetus to change and innovation, the modification of the Basketmakers was a significant move forward in the lifeway that was Anasazi. It was the era that tripped the latch and swung wide the gate to the future for a developing and dynamic civilization.

Eventually, as their Paleolithic ancestors had been, they were swallowed up by the larger group.

Basketmaker III

New varieties of beans and squash were among the plants that helped the people known as Basketmaker III make the transition to a settled lifestyle. Cotton also appeared about A.D. 500, probably introduced from the south. Although cotton had no effect on the food supply, its use greatly increased the quality of textiles, which previously depended on coarse fibers such as those from yucca leaves.

It was corn, however, in new varieties—larger, more nutritious, easier to grow—that made the change to settled lives possible. Chief among these new varieties was Maiz de Ocho, so called because each cob had eight rows of kernels—fewer than the chapalote but containing larger kernels that were softer and higher in nutritional value. In addition, Maiz de Ocho had a shorter growing season, important in the high-altitude Four Corners where winter tended to linger and autumn arrive early.

Other varieties followed, although studies of trash heaps point to a slow evolution rather than a sudden introduction. This suggests that the Anasazi may have learned to cross-pollinate varieties of corn in an effort to diversify their crops. The result was corn adapted to particular uses. Some corn could be roasted and eaten directly from the cob; other varieties were best for flour. Another variety was valued because it had a long, single taproot that could reach down to moisture deep in the soil.

Agriculture did, indeed, change the Anasazi's "visible and invisible" world, as Amsden wrote. One of the most striking features of the visible world were the first aboveground masonry structures in the Four Corners—meant not for people but for produce.

Agricultural peoples need as much surplus as possible to guard against poor harvests. As the Anasazi surpluses increased, they needed more storage space. Underground pits had been sufficient for the short term but were too vulnerable to moisture and vermin to be useful as permanent storage.

Larger Buildings

At first, these storage structures were small. Toward the end of the Basketmaker period, however, buildings were larger, and manos and metates have been found in the ruins, indicating that they might have been used for processing as well as storage.

The people continued to live in pithouses, but such dwellings changed along with the society. Basketmaker III pithouses were larger, and some contained more than one room. Some were rectangular instead of round. Some had benches along the perimeter and niches in the walls, perhaps for storage. These larger, multiroom pithouses point to a more communal way of living. They are thought to have housed multiple or extended families, early versions of clans.

Remains of the later pithouses also furnish clues as to how the "invisible" world of the Anasazi changed. They contained foot drums—cavities in the floor covered over with planks that produced a hollow sound when stamped upon. Even more indicative of an increase in ceremonial practices was the small hole in the floor—only a few inches across—symbolizing the *sipapu*, the place traditionally thought to connect this world to the underworld below.

The Basketmakers and their ancestors had probably always had some form of ceremonial religion intended, as Amsden wrote, "to keep pace with those mystic powers which control all of life on earth, powers lurking everywhere to bring poverty or plenty."[11] But while earlier ceremonies likely involved hunting, the focus is thought to have shifted to agriculture as the move to a settled lifestyle progressed.

Dependent on Nature

Farmers, tied to the land and to a single location as they were, were totally dependent on the forces of nature for their livelihood. They sought to maintain a balance, a harmony with those forces, which would guarantee adequate rainfall and plentiful harvests. Ceremonies reflecting each passing season of the year, held underground, within the earth from which the crops grew, would have been entirely appropriate.

Whether the late Basketmakers practiced such a cycle of ceremonies is not certain but is highly likely. Today's Pueblo tribes—direct descendants of the Anasazi—follow this pattern, one that their oral tradition says goes back to earliest times. Ceremonies vary, and elements have probably been added through contact with other peoples, but there is little doubt that the basic necessity of living in harmony with nature became the core of Anasazi religion.

Toward the end of the Basketmaker period, the pithouse *sipapu* vanished in some settlements, only to appear in other structures. These new structures still were round and underground but were apparently used exclusively for ceremonies. Scientists term them "protokivas," speculating that they represent the forerunner of the kiva, Hopi for "underground room," the subterranean ceremonial chamber featured in later Anasazi cities and still in use by the Pueblo tribes.

BASKETMAKER ROCK ART

The Anasazi had no written language, but they did leave behind for scientists to study petroglyphs and pictographs scratched into and painted on cliff faces. These images are known collectively as rock art.

Some people think rock art was a kind of language and have spent years attempting to translate it. Still others caution not to try to read too much into every symbol, some of which may amount to no more than prehistoric doodling.

Human or humanlike figures, however, probably were religious in nature, as Polly Schaafsma describes in *Houses Beneath the Rock*, edited by David Grant Noble:

They are abstract, remote, static forms, lacking human qualities. Their elaborate headgear is another clue to their supernatural affiliations. . . . Occasionally staring eyes and unnatural hands and feet are pictured. . . . [Also pictured are] numerous handprints, birds, and occasional snakes closely associated with these ethereal beings. The handprints are usually stamped near the figures, or they may be placed on their torsos or around the heads. Occasionally babies' footprints were also stamped on the rocks. The consistent association of handprints [with the humanoid figures] . . . suggests that they were made for some definite purpose. They may have been left as signatures of prayer requests or made in the act of obtaining power—either from the rock-art figure itself or from the place it occupied.

This petroglyph in Monument Valley, Arizona, shows a large antelope leaping as a smaller one stands still. Some experts believe petroglyphs were used as a kind of written language.

Some protokivas were the size of large pithouses and were probably used by family groups. Others were larger, as much as forty feet in diameter, and could have contained the population of entire villages. These large protokivas indicate a shift of the Anasazi toward communal rather than individual worship, and their discovery in the 1920s furnished the first direct link between the Basketmakers and the modern Pueblo.

New Pottery Forms

The increased emphasis on religion was reflected in the arts and crafts of the late Basketmakers. Pottery, once confined to household utensils, took on different shapes and colors. Ruins have yielded clay figurines of humans, animals, and some objects that elude identification. Some of the human figures had been pierced with thorns, leading to speculation that a form of witchcraft

may have been practiced. While the clay figures, as well as those painted and carved on cliff and canyon walls throughout the Four Corners, seem to have religious overtones, their exact meaning is unknown.

The late Basketmaker period was a time of great expansion as well as great change. In the Four Corners alone, more than nine hundred Basketmaker III settlements have been found—as compared with one hundred from Basketmaker II. The Anasazi expanded geographically as well, occupying an area stretching from the Rio Grande in New Mexico to the Arizona-Nevada border.

The Basketmaker period had seen the formation of the Anasazi, their transition to a farm and village life, and a formalization of religion. Various groups would not progress at the same pace, but all would soon take the next important step that would lead in only a few hundred years to the height of Anasazi civilization.

CHAPTER THREE

THE
FIRST PUEBLOS

In 700 A.D. the Anasazi were living in underground pithouses. Barely two hundred years later, they had begun building the "great houses" whose monumental ruins stand in mute testimony to their architectural genius. This pivotal time in their history comprises the first part of what scholars term the Pueblo period.

When Spanish explorers wandering through the Southwest in the 1540s saw the collections of multistory dwellings of the Zuni, Hopi, Tewa, and other tribes, they called them *pueblos*, the Spanish word for "villages." The name subsequently was applied to the many southwestern tribes widely considered by scientists—and by the natives themselves—to be the direct descendants of the Anasazi.

When anthropologists began discovering the various types of aboveground Anasazi villages, they immediately saw the similarity to contemporary Indian villages and in 1927 applied the word Pueblo to the entire time from A.D. 700 to the present. Initially, the period was divided into five segments:

Pueblo I
(A.D. 700–900)

Pueblo II
(A.D. 900–1100/1150)

Pueblo III
(A.D. 1100/1150–1200/1300)

Pueblo IV
(A.D. 1300–1600)

Pueblo V
(A.D. 1600–present)

The difficulty with this system, known as the Pecos classification, is the uncertainty about distinctions between Pueblo II and III, since the development of Anasazi architecture varied widely from place to place. In 1935, anthropologist Frank Roberts devised the more descriptive nomenclature that bears his name:

Developmental Pueblo
(A.D. 750–1100)

Great or Classic Pueblo
(A.D. 1100–1300)

Regressive Pueblo
(A.D. 1300–1600)

Historic Pueblo
(A.D. 1600–present)

Both classification systems remain in general use and, although scientists are not completely satisfied with either one, no one has improved on them.

The White House Ruin sits just above the floor of Canyon de Chelly in northeastern Arizona. This location was close to crops on the canyon floor but protected from flash floods.

During the extremely long time period known as the Pueblo, aboveground structures changed dramatically. Certainly, the earliest structures of Pueblo I bear little resemblance to modern villages. They were not masonry constructions, for example, but more like pithouses that had been moved above ground.

Jacal Construction

The first aboveground buildings, the storage rooms of the late Basketmaker period, were made by a method known as jacal. The walls consisted of upright wooden poles lashed together and plastered with mud or clay, with the roof of branches and twigs similarly covered. It was precisely the same technique as the aboveground part of a pithouse. Indeed, the mud or clay for plaster came from the digging of the pithouses that people were still constructing at that time.

Another type of aboveground structure was used—one that went back possibly to the late Archaic period. When people were working on various outdoor chores, whether grinding seeds or fashioning arrowheads, they needed protection from the blazing southwestern sun. The solution was the ra-

ROOTED IN THE PAST

The first people to study the imposing buildings left behind by the Anasazi concluded that they must have been inspired by the great civilizations of ancient Mexico—the Toltec, Maya, and Aztec. What was seen in the Four Corners, they said, was probably a crude imitation of what had been built to the south.

One of the later and most knowledgeable experts on the Anasazi, Charles Avery Amsden, took the view—now shared by most archaeologists—that the Anasazi great houses, while they might have had some Mexican influence, were mostly the product of the Anasazi themselves. Amsden wrote, as quoted in *Pueblo Children of the Earth Mother* by Thomas E. Mails,

> Pueblo architecture was largely, if not entirely, an indigenous growth, rooted literally enough in the sandy floor of the Basketmaker cave. Here, among the earliest Anasazi of which we have any knowledge, are such structural features as fitted stone walls mortared and spalled, partitions, contiguous walls, wall recesses forming benches, vaulted roofs, cross-beam roofs with supporting posts to carry their weight, adobe roof coverings, and hatchway entrances. Here is the pueblo in embryo.

mada, a simple, basic shelter consisting of four upright poles at the corners supporting a roof of branches and twigs.

The first aboveground dwelling may well have been little more than an enhanced ramada. An enclosed space was made simply by adding jacal walls to the basic ramada structure. Such a structure, however, by no means replaced the pithouse. Indeed, throughout much of the Pueblo period, pithouses existed alongside surface structures—even the early great houses.

Such a reluctance to abandon old ways was due to the fact that, despite the architectural innovations, Pueblo I and II were conservative times. Only about 250 new settlements were built, as compared with more than 900 during Basketmaker times. The number seems particularly modest when one considers that many of the newer settlements lasted for only thirty to forty years.

Worsening Climate

The conservatism of the Pueblo I and II people stemmed from the age-old problem of the region—an adverse change in climatic conditions. After the comparatively benign weather enjoyed by the late Basketmakers, the early Pueblo people saw rainfall decrease year by year. Moreover, when rain did come, it was often very heavy, only to be followed by months of drought. Underground water tables fell in lowland areas. Farmable soil was either blown or washed away.

Poor conditions in the lowlands forced the Anasazi to migrate to higher ground where rainfall was greater and more water was available from melting winter snow. Since the majority of the wild plants that had furnished a portion of the Basketmaker diet were at lower elevations, the Anasazi became more dependent than ever on domesticated crops.

It might be expected, under such poor conditions, that the early Pueblo villages would be smaller than those of the late Basketmakers. In fact, just the opposite is the case, the consequence of a need for security offered by greater numbers. Population had grown during the Basketmaker era, and the bad weather and resulting bad crops created a food shortage. For one of the few times in Anasazi history, there appears to have been internal warfare. Some of the ruins of smaller, very early Pueblo I sites show signs of having been overrun by enemies. Investigators have discovered bodies in burned-out dwellings, leading to speculation that some groups, desperate for food, attacked their more fortunate neighbors.

Larger Villages

People in larger numbers would have been much better able to resist attack. Later villages are much larger—fifteen to twenty pithouses rather than the earlier five to ten—and up to one hundred surface structures. Larger villages held larger populations; estimates range from five hundred to six hundred people.

In addition, the later settlements were more often built on ridges, outcroppings, against canyon walls, and in other locations more easily defended. Some of these villages had wooden palisades or stone walls, the first such in Anasazi history.

Taking such a settlement by storm would have been difficult, especially since weapons—the atlatl and the bow and arrow—were much more effective for hunting than for

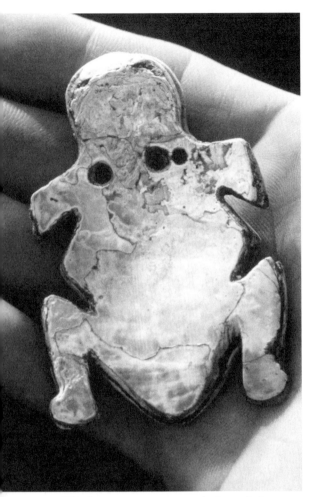

This frog ornament was made from abalone shell. The Anasazi acquired shells from as far away as California and the Texas coast.

attacking a walled settlement. Eventually, the early Pueblo Anasazi found another, less violent way to deal with periodic food shortages—trade.

The Anasazi had never lived in a vacuum. As far back as the Archaic period, for example, they were importing new forms of dart points developed by other peoples. Basketmaker bodies were sometimes buried with jewelry including shells that could have come only from the coasts of California or Texas. The most important innovations of the early Anasazi—corn, pottery, bow and arrow—came from other people, notably from the Hohokam and Mogollon just a few days' walk to the south.

The Six "Leagues"

Trade among Anasazi groups, however, was probably something new, although it is hard to be sure, since goods made by the Basketmakers were uniform across the entire region. During the Pueblo period, however, cultural diversity developed among the Anasazi. Gradually, through migration and the drawing together into larger settlements, six loosely confederated Anasazi "leagues," as anthropologists have called them, developed. These included the Virgin Anasazi in the area of the Virgin River in southwestern Utah and northwestern Arizona, the Kayenta in northeastern Arizona, Mesa Verde in southwestern Colorado, Chaco in northwestern New Mexico, Little Colorado along the Little Colorado River in eastern Arizona, and Rio Grande along the Rio Grande in north-central New Mexico.

The respective leagues were not unified as an individual tribe would be, and the people probably never considered themselves part of any such group. Nevertheless, geographical and slight climatic differences caused them to develop, at different times, distinct lifestyles, arts, and architecture.

It was variation in one primary area—pottery—that fueled trade during Pueblo I and II. Anasazi pottery continued through the entire Pueblo period to be almost exclusively black and white or gray and white, just as it had been throughout the Basket-maker period. Gradually, however, a divergence in style occurred between groups in the Northwest and those in the Southeast areas.

Pots from Kayenta and Mesa Verde in the Northwest had highly polished, white surfaces with designs in gray-black. Kayenta also produced distinctive black-on-red pottery. To the southeast, pottery had a chalky, white surface with red-black paint designs.

The designs themselves were much the same—a few basic geometrical figures repeated and used in combination. Anasazi pottery showed little of the free-form innovation of other southwestern peoples and reflected the conservatism of Pueblo I and II. Indeed, most pottery of the Anasazi's modern Pueblo descendants tended to follow very rigid, traditional forms until the twentieth century when more experimentation began.

Trading Pottery

To the Anasazi, however, the regional differences between pottery were very significant, and works from other regions were highly prized. So it was that in a time when erratic rainfall might mean plentiful crops in one area and potential famine in another, pottery became a form of currency to trade for corn.

Pueblo I had little in the way of new crops. It was not a time for innovation, and

The ruins of Pueblo Bonito in Chaco Canyon, New Mexico, show a typical great house arrangement. The multistory living quarters faced a large plaza that featured large kivas.

what experimentation was done involved trying to produce corn that would be resistant to drought and that could adapt to the shorter growing season of the uplands.

Storing as much corn as possible was so important that aboveground storage rooms increased in size and sophistication. Where raw materials were available, stone masonry began to replace jacal. The type of masonry depended on what materials were at hand. Kayenta and Mesa Verde had plenty of sandstone blocks that could be stacked and chinked with mud. In Chaco, the sandstone tended to be in slabs rather than blocks. The Rio Grande area was short of natural stone, so the builders made bricks of adobe, which is mud mixed with straw.

Eventually, for reasons either of convenience, security, or a combination of the two, the Pueblo I people adopted the practice of living next to their food supply. Multiroom structures appeared, usually a front room used as the residence, complete with a fire pit for cooking, and a rear room for food storage. Pithouses remained nearby, however, and the Anasazi probably retreated to them in colder weather.

Sometime in the 800s, the architectural innovation took place that would eventually reach its peak expression in the great houses of Chaco Canyon and the spectacular cliff dwellings of Mesa Verde. The stand-alone, two-room houses of Pueblo I began to be placed adjacent to one another, sharing a common wall. This could have been because such structures were easier to build, but more likely it was because members of a family began adding rooms as needed. The change toward this type of settlement, which took place at various times in different localities, marked the start of Pueblo II.

Multiroom Complexes

As Pueblo II progressed, the multiroom complexes became larger. One of the most common types was six two-room houses in a straight line. Later, another row might be started at a right angle to the first, resulting in an L-shaped structure. In some cases, the complex took on a U shape when a third row was built.

Sometimes, the rows of houses were not built piecemeal, adding a house at a time, but as a single complex. In many such cases, the rows were not straight but in an arc. This was particularly true in the Chaco area and would set the pattern for the first great houses. Some Pueblo II houses had exterior doors, but openings in the roof continued to be the favorite method of entry and exit. Roofs also became more substantial to the point where they could be used as areas for household activities to take place.

The area in front of the housing rows or within the U shape or arc was used for community activities and became the plaza. In good weather, the people might gather there, chatting with one another to make the time pass—the women to grind corn or paint pottery and the men to make arrowheads. The plaza became an integral part of Anasazi architecture and remains a feature of modern pueblos.

During Pueblo II, fewer pithouses were built, although some people continued to live in older ones. Underground structures, however, remained important. Some small pithouses near the larger houses show signs of residential use, but most of the underground chambers—kivas—were used for ceremonial activities by this time.

The number of kivas depended on the size of the village. Larger villages might have two or more smaller kivas that some anthropologists have called "clan" kivas. Such a term is a bit misleading, however. Although these rooms were probably used by family groups, there is no evidence that clans existed in the sense used by the Pueblo today.

Large Kivas

In addition to these clan kivas, many villages had much larger ceremonial rooms, large enough to hold the entire settlement's population. These might have been used for religious ceremonies in which the people of all families—or more likely only the men—would gather.

Naturally, architecture depended on location. The caves of the Mesa Verde and Kayenta areas, for example, lent themselves more to straight-line construction than to curved rows. Sometimes the earth was so hard and rocky that kivas were built above ground.

Pueblo II saw a dramatic increase in the number of new settlements, an estimated ten thousand between A.D. 850 and 1000. Many of these, however, might be occupied for only a couple of generations before lack of rainfall forced the group to move on. These villages, while more architecturally sophisticated than those of Pueblo I, tended to be smaller. Overall population had grown to the point where it could not be supported by existing sites with good water supplies. Family groups had to strike out in search of new sites where there might be enough rainfall to support a smaller settlement.

This large kiva is part of the Chimney Rock Ruins at Pagosa Springs, Colorado. Large kivas may have been used for community ceremonies, while smaller ones were reserved for families or clans.

Farming More Land

Farming had undergone some changes since Pueblo I. Despite the general conservatism of the period, the Anasazi had continued to experiment with different types of corn. New types of squash and beans also appeared. Rainfall, though still inconsistent, was at least more plentiful than it had been, making the increase in the number of villages possible.

This expansion put more land under cultivation than in any other period in Anasazi history, before or since. They used almost every possible piece of land, writes anthropologist Linda Cordell, "avoiding only flood plains during times when they were being buried by streams depositing quantities of sediment onto them."[12]

To trap and use every bit of precious water, they began to develop irrigation systems. The earliest were simple check dams, walls of stone or earth placed across drainages to channel water toward crops. Late in Pueblo II, especially in Chaco Canyon, farmers employed terraced fields and an intricate system of canals to catch water running down canyon walls.

The tremendous progress made by the Anasazi during the Pueblo I and II periods came with a price—hard work. Expansion of farmland had brought about a corresponding scarcity of game. Examination of human coprolite, or dried fecal matter, shows that the diet was as high as 85 percent corn, meaning there was a dependency on agriculture as never before.

Everyone old enough to work in the fields did so, and those not old enough to work were taken there anyway. It was during early Pueblo times that women began strapping babies into cradle boards and taking them everywhere they went.

About A.D. 900 another change began to take place among the Anasazi. While most settlements remained of the Pueblo II type, concentrating on raising and storing as much food as possible, others began to grow far larger—hundreds of rooms instead of a dozen or so. The dawn of the Classic Pueblo period had arrived.

CHAPTER FOUR

THE GREAT PUEBLOS

The great flowering of Anasazi civilization was the Pueblo III, or Classic Pueblo period. Only three of the six Anasazi regions, however, experienced this phenomenon. The building boom touched the Virgin Anasazi hardly at all. Large pueblos were built in both the Little Colorado and Rio Grande regions, but these came after the Classic period and were, for the most part, only echoes of the greatness seen at Chaco Canyon, Mesa Verde, and Kayenta.

The logical place to begin any discussion is with Chaco, whose name comes from the Navajo for "rock canyon." It was the earliest and grandest, and it heavily influenced the later development of its neighbors.

Many writers marvel that anything could ever bloom in Chaco Canyon, describing the place as arid and bleak. Others say that how one views Chaco Canyon depends on one's viewpoint. Archaeologist Arthur Kidder wrote that Chaco's detractors "have failed to realize the ability of the Pueblo Indian to support himself quite comfortably in the face of conditions of dryness that would stagger the white farmer."[13]

A Remote Location

And yet, it remains difficult to understand, walking through this scrubby, almost barren area of northwestern New Mexico, how anyone could survive there, much less make it the center of a flourishing civilization. Even in a time when a grid of superhighways has brought everything and everyone closer, Chaco Canyon is remote—fifty miles from the nearest sizable town and accessible only after seventeen bone-jarring miles over a corrugated dirt road.

Of course, the landscape was not always the way it is now. Three years before he discovered Cliff Palace at Mesa Verde, Richard Wetherill visited Chaco Canyon and noted that "grass and water is plenty—wood is scarce."[14] Even in better circumstances, however, the Chaco area could not have supported the number of people thought to have lived there.

The Chacoan civilization is so unlike anything that preceded it among the Anasazi that scientists have long surmised its founders came from elsewhere. Early investigators claimed it was the northernmost outpost of the Toltec empire in Mexico. More recently, other experts have suggested that the ancestors of the people who built the great houses migrated from southwestern Colorado and southeastern Utah. Since traces of some Basketmaker and Pueblo I dwellings have been found, however, the possibility remains that

Pueblo Bonito, one of the most elaborate Anasazi great houses, nestles against the wall of Chaco Canyon, New Mexico. The complex had more than eight hundred rooms and thirty-three kivas.

the seeds of such rapid development might have been present in Chaco Canyon all along. Finally, unable to come up with an adequate explanation for what occurred, scientists have dubbed it the Chaco phenomenon.

Foremost among the many striking features of the Chacoan great houses is their sheer size, especially compared with Pueblo II complexes, which might have 20 rooms at the most. The great houses in and around the canyon had an average of 216 rooms, and the largest great house to have been excavated, Pueblo Bonito, Spanish for "beautiful village," had more than 800 rooms and 33 kivas, including 2 "great kivas" more than forty feet in diameter.

Excavation of Pueblo Bonito was begun in 1896 by a team headed by Richard Wether-

ill. After four years, almost 200 rooms had been uncovered and almost seventy thousand artifacts shipped to the American Museum of Natural History in New York. One government observer, S.J. Holsinger, called Pueblo Bonito the "ruin of ruins, the equal of which in point of magnitude and general interest, is not to be found among the world's collection of discovered prehistoric structures."[15]

In fact, Pueblo Bonito is not even the largest great house in the annals of Chacoan civilization. Remote sensing devices mounted in airplanes have revealed massive sites miles to the northwest that may be larger. One, near Newcomb, New Mexico, has not been excavated but may contain as many as 1,250 rooms.

Growth by Design

Another feature that makes the Chaco great houses so intriguing is that they were designed from the outset to be large. Pueblo II complexes had grown room by room. Later Anasazi great houses would grow much the same way—suites of rooms built next to others as the need arose. The

THE T-SHAPED DOORS

One of the more puzzling aspects of Anasazi architecture are the T-shaped doors found at Chaco Canyon and Mesa Verde. They are found mostly on exterior doors but also on some doors connecting interior rooms. They occur far less frequently than other door openings, but they are taller.

At the bottom, these doors are about two feet across. Then, perhaps three feet from the floor, they expand at right angles to a width of about three feet.

Pueblo Indian guides suggested to archaeologists that the wider upper part of the doorways would have made it far easier to carry bundles of firewood indoors, but that does not explain why only some exterior doors are T-shaped and why some of the doors are interior.

Another possible explanation is that the bottom half could be covered, making the top half into a window. Conversely, the top half could be covered, turning the bottom half into a ventilator for the fire pit. Again, neither of these explanations covers interior doors.

In *A.D. 1250*, Lawrence W. Cheek speculates, "An exotic idea is that the form echoes the Mesoamerican water deity Tlaloc, whose T-like image surfaces in many Pan-American cultures. The uniquely shaped entrance is typically found, it has been suggested, only with rooms associated with certain ceremonial functions."

T-shaped doors, such as this one at Pueblo Bonito in Chaco Canyon, appeared in many Anasazi great houses.

builders of the Chaco great houses, however, were working from a plan. Stories were set back from one another in a precise pattern. Bottom-story walls were built extra thick, obviously because they were intended to bear the weight of construction above.

This is not to say that the great houses were built all at once. Pueblo Bonito was begun in the early 900s and went through several phases before its completion about 1067. The plan underwent several alterations, with rooms and even sacred kivas demolished to make way for larger structures.

Another distinctive feature of Chaco architecture, in addition to scale and planning, is the high degree of skill developed by the Anasazi masons. The walls of Pueblo Bonito and its sister great houses show degrees of expertise that would not be equaled in the other Anasazi regions, even though they would come hundreds of years later.

Chacoan Masonry

The Chaco cities featured four distinct styles of masonry. The oldest walls, known as Old Bonitan, were simple and rudimentary, flat slabs of sandstone set irregularly in a mud mortar, much like the walls of Pueblo II houses. Next came the first of three Late Bonitan styles in what is called core and veneer. The interior of the wall was the same sandstone and mud as before, but after completion it was faced on both sides with carefully selected and shaped, or "dressed," sandstone.

Type I Late Bonitan walls featured rows of dressed sandstone blocks of various sizes mortared together with small sandstone chips chinked between the rows. In Type II, the rows were made up of uniform dressed blocks and separated with bands made up of much thinner sandstone slabs. In Type III, the uniform blocks were laid in rows with a minimum of mortar and no chinking, in much the same manner as a modern brick wall. Sometimes blocks of various colors were set in patterns.

Chacoan masons possessed an eye for beauty and regularity of design in addition to a sound grasp of architectural engineering. Thus, it is all the more amazing to the modern observer that these stone veneers,

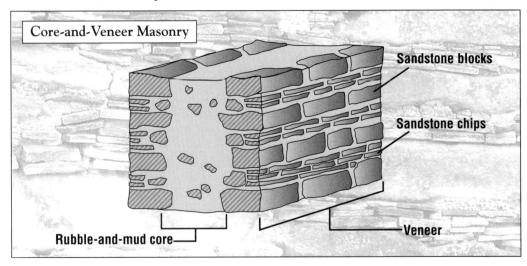

Core-and-Veneer Masonry

Sandstone blocks

Sandstone chips

Veneer

Rubble-and-mud core

A roof at Pueblo Bonito shows how the Anasazi were able to cover large interior areas without central support pillars. The technique of laying logs at angles to one another is called cribbing.

once they were painstakingly completed, were plastered over with mud or clay. The fact that the masons used such precise techniques on a wall to be plastered speaks eloquently to their pride in workmanship.

The Chaco Anasazi kivas also were architectural wonders. Even the two great kivas of Pueblo Bonito seem small compared to their nearby neighbor at Casa Rinconada, the largest of the Anasazi kivas with a diameter of 62.5 feet. The builders needed considerable ingenuity and engineering skill to roof over such a huge area and did so by building four large pillars, then laying beams on them to form a rectangular base. The design was much like the ancient pithouse roof but on a vastly larger scale.

Roof Cribbing

In smaller kivas, such freestanding support pillars would have taken too much room. The builders solved this problem by placing the pillars against the walls, laying logs from one to the other, then laying slightly smaller logs across the angle made by the first ones. This technique, called cribbing, produced a dome-shaped roof.

So much construction naturally required an immense amount of building material. More than 50 million dressed stones and an estimated twenty-five thousand trees went into the building of Pueblo Bonito alone. Obtaining sandstone was no problem, since it lay on the canyon floor in abundance. The trees were another matter altogether.

Importing Materials

Juniper and willow were available, but their branches were too thin to be used for anything but matting. Both the primary beams (*vigas*) and secondary crosspieces (*latias*), then, are of wood not found at Chaco. Pine, ash, and spruce had to be cut in distant forests and then transported—quite a feat considering the Anasazi had neither horses nor wheeled vehicles. For example, the giant Ponderosa pine *vigas*, weighing several hundred pounds each, had to be carried by men from the Chuska Mountains, thirty miles to the west.

In addition to having few trees, the Chacoans had little water, but they were highly innovative in their use of irrigation systems. They had no reliable source of water, since Chaco Wash, which bisects the canyon floor, is dry most of the year. Instead, they built a sophisticated system of dams to catch runoff.

Yet even with such novel irrigation systems, the fields in and around the canyon were probably insufficient to grow the amount of food needed to support the population. One theory is that the "outliers," as the Chacoan cities far from the canyon were called, were created to grow crops for the cities in the canyon, to act as "breadbaskets" for what amounted to a capital city.

Many Rooms, Few People

Another theory, and one increasingly in favor with anthropologists, is that the population of Chaco Canyon simply was never all that large to begin with. The great complexes and other dwellings on the floor of the canyon and just above the canyon rim were capable of housing about thirty thousand people. Pueblo Bonito, if fully occupied, could have held about two thousand people.

The key phrase is "if fully occupied." While there are hundreds of rooms at Pueblo Bonito and the other great houses, few seemed to have been lived in. For example, only a handful of rooms, usually those facing the exterior, have fire pits, and even some of those appear to have been infrequently occupied. Some experts suggest that there may have been as few as forty permanent residents. Of the hundreds of other rooms, many were no doubt used for storage, but researchers using sensitive equipment have turned up no trace of corn pollen in many more. What, then, were they used for?

This mystery is only one piece of a larger puzzle—what was the Chaco phenomenon? Why were these huge buildings constructed in an unlikely location to house a relatively small number of people?

A Trading Center

David Stuart points out that Chaco Canyon was on the boundary between two southwestern rainfall patterns, one depending on late summer rains and the other on winter rain or snow. He suggests that, given the emphasis on trade in the Developmental Pueblo period, Chaco could have become a center for the collection, storage, and distribution of corn.

The notion of Chaco as a trading center is bolstered by the large number of artifacts found there that originated in Mexico—copper bells, parrot and macaw feathers—and some architectural features. Such finds suggest that contacts with the Toltec civilization, from which such items likely originated, may have spurred the unprecedented building boom.

Such an explanation of Chaco is little more than supposition built on speculation built on very little hard evidence. What is certain, however, is that the Chaco phenomenon could not sustain itself. The pace of building slowed and finally, about 1130, stopped altogether. The population decreased. One by one, villages were abandoned, as were large sections of the great houses. By 1200, Chaco

LIFE AT CHACO CANYON

While archaeologists and anthropologists usually stick to the facts and what can be proven beyond doubt by their research, they cannot help sometimes allowing their imaginations to come to the forefront. In Gene S. Stuart's *America's Ancient Cities*, noted archaeologist Linda Cordell pictures what daily life might have been like in Chaco Canyon:

> As the Anasazi tended their crops, traders went from village to village, offering news and gossip as well as their wares. Occasionally, perhaps, traders from the far south were drawn to the bustling towns, offering scarlet-winged macaws for turquoise tessera or beads. At times, processions of men in finely woven kilts and heavy necklaces of shell may have entered the plazas to the measured rhythms of flutes and drums to offer dances for rain and for the good of all the people. . . . While they [men and boys] worked, they would recite and discuss the traditional stories and legends that contained the truths of the Anasazi way of life—the ways of the gods and the ancestors, the habits of mammals and birds, the etiquette of social life, and the organization of the universe.

Canyon was all but deserted, and the story of the Anasazi had moved north and west to Mesa Verde and Kayenta.

Mesa Verde

Say "Anasazi" and most people immediately picture the great cliff houses at Mesa Verde National Park—and with good reason. Set against the sweep of the cliffs, a carpet of junipers and piñon pine at their feet, glowing softly in the late afternoon sun, they have been one of the most enduring symbols of the American West for more than a century. As magnificent as they are, however, they cannot compare with those at Chaco in size, technical skill required to build them, or length of habitation. Indeed, of the seven-hundred-year history of the Anasazi at Mesa Verde, the Classic Pueblo period spanned only the last seventy-five to one hundred years.

During the rest of their tenure—from the earliest Basketmaker pithouses of about A.D. 600 through Pueblo II—the Mesa Verdeans lived on top of the mesa, near their farms. Throughout most of the 1000s and 1100s, the pinnacle of building at Chaco Canyon, only a few large communities were built, and few of these housed more than two hundred people.

Architecture was similar to Pueblo II sites elsewhere, except for the presence of three- to four-story towers. These towers may have been used as lookout posts, since the Mesa Verdeans were much closer than their Chaco kin were to potential enemies, such as the Utes. However, since the towers were usually next to kivas, their purpose may have been religious, perhaps to observe the heavens.

Moving Below

At the end of the 1100s the Mesa Verdeans began to move off the mesa top and into the canyons below, where they built the famous cliff houses. Why they did so remains a mystery. Some have suggested a religious motivation, always a possibility in light of what is known of the spiritual aspects of Anasazi life. Others think that perhaps it was because the caves offered better shelter, although the winters were no more severe than before. The prevailing theory, however, is that the Mesa Verdeans felt threatened by external enemies. One sign pointing in this direction was the building of walls around late

Balcony House at Mesa Verde, Colorado, shows how the Anasazi shaped multistory towers to fit the shape of caves. Such structures were built without the aid of nails, bolts, or metal tools.

Pueblo II villages and the movement of kivas inside these walls.

Certainly, whatever their motivation, it must have seemed compelling for the Anasazi to abandon the mesa tops and go to the enormous trouble of building the cliff houses. While the Mesa Verdeans had an advantage over the Chaco Anasazi in that they had plenty of wood in addition to stone, the problem was getting the materials to the building site.

Narrow, twisting pathways lead to some Mesa Verde cliff houses, but most could only be reached with rope ladders or by climbing down the face of the cliff using niches hacked out of the rock. It was a dangerous enough process unencumbered, let alone with a load of materials or tools strapped to one's back.

The Anasazi took advantage of almost every available spot. Of the estimated six hundred cliff houses, the large majority have fewer than 20 rooms and some are large enough only for a single family. The largest, Cliff Palace, with its 220 rooms and 33 kivas, is smaller than the Chacoan great houses. The builders might have wanted larger complexes, but the caves simply did not offer enough room.

Different Plans

Refugees from Chaco Canyon may have influenced the builders at Mesa Verde, but the great houses are very different in ways other than size. Rather than being planned as large complexes, the Mesa Verde houses grew by accretion. That is, after the first suites of rooms were built, others were tacked on as new families moved from the mesa top. The large number of kivas as compared with rooms suggests that the population was more a collection of small clans rather than a large, unified community.

Interestingly, the towers of the mesa-top towns were repeated in the cliff houses. This makes it more likely that they had a religious function, since their canyon location would have given them little value as lookout posts.

Masonry at Mesa Verde was also far different from that at Chaco. Builders were far less painstaking with wall veneers, which appear somewhat crude when compared to those of Chaco, even though Chaco's date from more than a century earlier. The sandstone blocks are more or less uniform but are less consistent in size and shape.

Unlike at Chaco Canyon, the Mesa Verde great houses were probably fully occupied, except for storage rooms. This would have resulted in a peak population in A.D. 1250 of about twenty thousand people. Fifty years later, however, the magnificent sites were completely deserted.

Kayenta

The story was much the same at Kayenta, only on a much smaller scale. If so sparsely settled an area as the Four Corners could have had an area that was a quiet backwater by comparison, Kayenta qualified. The mesa tops get far less rainfall than at Mesa Verde, and the land is scored by deep, twisting chasms, including, on the area's western edge, the Grand Canyon.

The Kayenta Anasazi farmed the mesa tops through the Basketmaker and Developmental Pueblo periods, but an extended drought in the mid-1100s forced them to change. They moved their farms to the canyon floors, but while the land there was good for farming, it was an impossible place to live. First, it was hot, the temperatures well above those on the mesas, with little wind to offer relief from the heat. Second, the canyon floors were much narrower than those in the Chaco region. The heavy late summer rains would have resulted in flash floods, washing away any structure. The Kayentans, like their Mesa Verde cousins, found their solution in cliff houses. Starting about 1150 they began to build in caves situated far enough above the canyon floor to provide safety from flooding.

The best-known Kayentan buildings, Betatakin and Keet Seel in northeastern Arizona, were begun about 1250. At Betatakin, three-room suites were added until 1280 when the peak population of about 125 persons was reached. Keet Seel was the largest of the Kayentan houses but had only 155 rooms and housed perhaps 150 persons.

KAYENTA

Most of the attention of tourists as well as scientists is directed at two of the three major Anasazi sites, Chaco Canyon and Mesa Verde. The third, Kayenta, does not seem to have gone in for building on quite the same scale, although the ruins of Betatakin and Keet Seel are spectacular.

Donald G. Pike, in *Anasazi: Ancient People of the Rock*, says that the Kayenta Anasazi, because of the ruggedness of the land they inhabited, were more concerned with daily living than with monumental building:

> Among the world of the Anasazi, Kayenta constituted what seems now to have been a quiet backwater of cultural growth. The sophisticated innovations of Mesa Verde and Chaco were adopted slowly and deliberately, the people absorbing possibly more than they originated. With a charming disregard for the diction that "newer is better," they mixed the old building technique of wattle-and-daub with the more advanced pure stone masonry, continued to live in freestanding pueblos right next to the cliff dwelling at Keet Seel, and took their religion in smaller doses, avoiding the compulsive kiva-building that characterized Chaco especially. They were not lethargic bumpkins, country cousins to the true way; rather they were people faced with survival in a harder land, devoting their energies to the demands of the digging stick and the hunt, fulfilling the basic needs of life first, and adding the veneer and filigree of civilization as time permitted.

Keet Seel, one of the largest great houses of the Kayenta Anasazi, was begun in 1250. Built over a period of twenty-five years, it was deserted by 1300.

Construction was crude compared with that at Chaco and Mesa Verde. Walls were seldom more than one stone block in thickness, and the stones were irregularly shaped and required large amounts of mortar. "From our perspective," writes Linda Cordell, "the Kayenta Anasazi were rather indifferent architects and masons."[16] Certainly the finest of their cliff dwellings fall far short of Chaco and Mesa Verde in almost every respect.

Kayenta Pottery

While they may not have been equal to other Anasazi as builders, the Kayentans excelled as potters. There is more variety in Kayentan pottery than in any other region. Their black-on-white pottery was the equal of any other group's, and they experi-

mented much more with color, taking advantage of the availability of different types of clay. Some experts declare Kayentan black-on-red the finest of all Anasazi pottery.

The bloom of Kayenta withered even more quickly than that at Mesa Verde. Building at Betatakin and Keet Seel, begun in 1250, ended about 1275. By 1300, about the same time as at Mesa Verde, the canyons and mesas were deserted, bringing an end to the Classic Pueblo period.

The pinnacle of Anasazi civilization had lasted only about 250 years. While their golden age lasted, however, the Anasazi provided a rich heritage of ritual, crafts, architecture, and the skills of everyday living that would be invaluable to their descendants.

CHAPTER FIVE

RITUAL AND RELIGION

Religion was, in all probability, the central focus of Anasazi life. Dependent as they were on the forces of nature, they doubtless took every measure possible to influence those forces to bring rain and healthy crops. While precise details of Anasazi ritual are sketchy at best, much can be inferred from the practices of their descendants, the Pueblo Indians. Thomas E. Mails writes,

> [Religion] has always been, and is still, the hub, the leaven, and the hope of [Pueblo] society. It binds them together now, and it is the cord that ties them inexorably to the ancient ways. The [modern] Anasazi Pueblos live their religion. . . . It is a religion that serves both community and personal needs, although the people make no distinction between the two.[17]

In Basketmaker times, the emphasis of religious practice was more on the individual than the community. Hunting was usually a solitary pursuit, and, if modern practice is a guide, the hunter went through a ritual to bring himself into a kind of spiritual harmony with his quarry. Likewise, farms were small and farmers moved often, and may have thought more about going

where the rainfall was rather than trying to make rainfall come to them. At any rate, until late in the period the Basketmakers did not build any structures that would point to community ceremonies.

The Basketmakers did, however, believe in some kind of afterlife, their modern name deriving from burial practice. Experts think the baskets placed over the heads of the deceased may have represented the world in which they lived. Baskets used in burials were "killed." That is, they had a hole punched through the bottom. The hole would represent the *sipapu*, the difference being that instead of emerging, the soul could return to the underworld through the orifice.

Grave Goods

In addition to baskets, people were buried with items that were likely intended to see them on their supernatural journey. Some, like sandals or weapons, were practical. The significance of other items—stuffed birds' heads, feathers, whistles—can only be guessed at. Bodies were drawn up with knees touching the chest, perhaps with the thought that the position that people took in the womb should be used when they left the world as well.

With the coming of the Developmental Pueblo period and the shift to a more settled agricultural economy, knowing exactly when to plant became extremely important. As a consequence, ceremonies likely evolved based on the seasons of the year. Someone had to keep track of the seasons, whether by observing the movements of the sun or the phases of the moon. Whether the local shaman, or medicine man, took on these additional duties, or whether the astronomers developed into shamans is not known.

It was probably not until the Classic Pueblo period that a class of full-time priests or religious leaders developed. Scientists examining burials in Chaco Canyon discovered that bodies in the great houses such as Pueblo Bonito were less numerous than in nearby smaller villages and had been interred with more and finer ornaments, including turquoise and shells seldom found in the more modest sites. Such burials tended to support the notion that the Chaco great houses were reserved for an elite group. These people could well have acted not only as priests but also as overseers of whatever distribution and trade system might have existed. Giving religious significance to trading corn as well as growing it would have been likely, in light of the emphasis modern Pueblo place on corn in their rituals.

This religious aspect of agriculture, some experts think, may have made Chaco Canyon a spiritual as well as economic center. The Chaco Canyon cities were only a part, although the most important part, of the vast Chacoan civilization. More than a hundred other sites, some as far away as one hundred miles, display use of the same architectural techniques. Their ruins yield the same kinds of pottery and other artifacts. Their construction began later than their counterparts in

This detailed human figure may have had some religious significance, but little is known about the specific rituals of the Anasazi.

the canyon, and experts were long unsure if they were built by people copying the Chacoans or by the Chacoans themselves as they expanded.

The question was answered dramatically in 1979 when the same remote sensing device that found new settlements revealed a network of roadways. These roads, 240 miles of them, went out in all directions from Chaco Canyon. Some went to major outliers. One led straight to the Chuska Mountains and could have been used to transport tree trunks used in construction.

Mystery of the Roads

The purpose of the roads, however, remains a mystery because of the way they were built. They were usually about thirty feet in width and ran, wherever possible, in a straight line. If a change of direction was required, the road made an angle instead of a curve. The builders scraped off surface soil

THE ROADS OF CHACO

One of the most puzzling features in the entire Anasazi area is the network of ancient roadways leading in all directions from Chaco Canyon. Ever since the roads were discovered in 1979, scientists have been questioning why the Chacoans, who had no horses or wheeled vehicles, would need such wide roads or, indeed, any roads at all.

The favorite explanation, given the prevalent idea that Chaco might have served as a regional distribution center as well as the focus of Anasazi religion, is that the roads were used for ceremonial purposes and to impress people of outlying communities. Dabney Ford, an archaeologist at Chaco Culture National Historical Park, explains in *America's Ancient Cities* by Gene S. Stuart:

> We once thought the roads were purely functional economic structures. We studied how many calories it took to walk on the desert as opposed to walking on roads. There wasn't much difference! Now we think the roads are just incredibly fancy—straight for no purpose. They lead to the edge of a cliff and a stairway when just ten feet in another direction there is a natural way to get down the cliff. Maybe long, wide roads were built to impress the people coming to Chaco. The planning and labor that went into these roads and towns is impressive. We're impressed today. There's no reason why someone a thousand years ago wouldn't have been.

to get to harder material underneath. The surface soil was put to either side, forming curbs. Sometimes the roads stop at the foot of a cliff and continue on the top, connected by a staircase hacked out of the stone face.

Certainly these roads could have been used by messengers or traders, or to transport building materials, but why the Chacoan Anasazi, with no horses and no wagons, would need such wide roads continues to puzzle scientists. They are also at a loss to explain why the great road leading north from the canyon is actually two pairs of parallel roads only one hundred feet apart.

If Chaco, indeed, was the religious center for all the Anasazi, the roads might have had religious significance. The growing of corn—the annual cycle of planting, tending, harvesting, and grinding and the eternal dependence on rain—is at the center of modern Pueblo religions and probably was for the Anasazi. The roads might have been made for large processions and the great houses to serve as dormitories for huge festivals or ceremonies. The few people who lived in Chaco Canyon year-round might have been members of an elite group, probably priests, who oversaw most aspects of religion, trade, and building. If so, however, this marked a departure for the Anasazi, who had lived for centuries with little sign of social class differences.

Hereditary Priesthood

This priesthood located at Chaco Canyon may have been hereditary. The fact that some of the bodies of children were buried with large amounts of turquoise suggests this. However, it is impossible to say whether these were children of the priests or children who had been taken from elsewhere to be trained as priests.

The key functions of the priestly caste seem to have been to keep calendars and use them to regulate the various aspects of agriculture and the ceremonies associated with them. Some of the uppermost rooms—five stories high—of the Chaco great houses were used neither for living nor for storage. In fact, they may have been used as observatories. These, plus the towers of Mesa Verde, lead some experts to think that the priests plotted the movements of the sun, moon, and stars to track seasonal changes and even predict eclipses. While there is little direct evidence that the Anasazi used the stars or planets in their ordering of the ceremonial year, experts think it is likely, since such practices have been documented among modern Pueblo Indians.

Of all the heavenly bodies, the sun was the most important to the Anasazi. Like many early civilizations the Anasazi used its movements to divide the year. The dividing points were the winter and summer solstices—the shortest and longest days of the year—and the vernal and autumnal equinoxes—the days in spring and fall when day and night are exactly the same length.

Careful Alignment

The priests used various means to track the sun's movements. Some of the great houses themselves were carefully planned to align precisely east-west. Scientists speculate that the priests may have used such alignments to pinpoint dates a few days prior to the autumnal equinox so that appropriate ceremonies could begin.

A ladder through the roof provided access to the kiva. The huge roof beams weighed several hundred pounds each and were often transported from distant forests.

Kivas also may have been used as indicators of the seasons. These ceremonial structures were also carefully aligned and, while no great kiva roof has been found intact, some experts think that the roof holes, used as entrances and for ventilation, could also have acted as calendars. Sunlight coming through the hole would have formed a bright spot on the kiva floor, and the spot would have moved across the floor each day in different lines as the sun rose and set at different places.

The most famous of all Anasazi astronomical features, however, are the Sun Daggers in Chaco Canyon discovered in 1977. Fajada Butte rises three hundred feet from the floor of the canyon at its southern end. High on one shoulder of the butte ancient astronomers set three vertical sandstone slabs in such a way that sunlight shining between them projects two shafts, or "daggers," onto the cliff face.

Marking the Solstices

Each day, as the sun moves across the sky, the daggers move across two spirals cut into the cliff face. Observing for two years the position of the daggers when the sun was directly overhead, archaeologists found that the summer solstice is marked by a dagger through the center of the large spiral, the winter solstice by daggers touching each side of the large spiral, and the equinoxes by a dagger through the center of the smaller spiral.

In addition to marking the solstices and equinoxes, the Sun Daggers can be used to track cycles of the moon and to predict lunar eclipses. In Thomas Mails's opinion, the

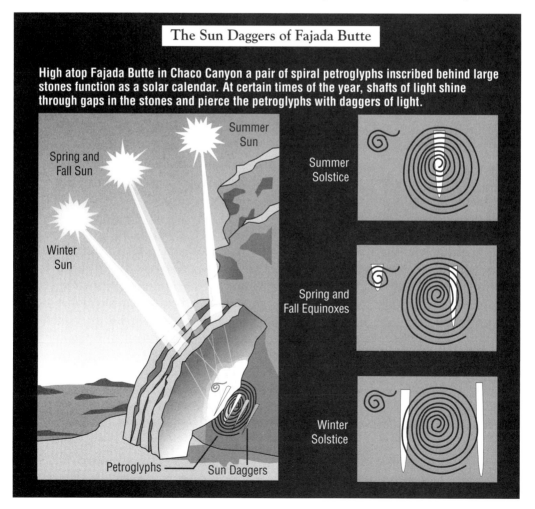

The Sun Daggers of Fajada Butte

High atop Fajada Butte in Chaco Canyon a pair of spiral petroglyphs inscribed behind large stones function as a solar calendar. At certain times of the year, shafts of light shine through gaps in the stones and pierce the petroglyphs with daggers of light.

Spring and Fall Sun

Summer Sun

Winter Sun

Summer Solstice

Spring and Fall Equinoxes

Winter Solstice

Petroglyphs — Sun Daggers

formation "ranks in precision, accuracy, and functional versatility with the best astronomical structures yet found in the Old and New worlds" and demonstrates that "the Anasazi and other ancient peoples of North America were far more sophisticated and knowledgeable than previously thought."[18]

The Fajada Sun Daggers, however, may have had much more significance than their use as an astronomical tool. Like so much in the Anasazi and Pueblo worlds, they are thought to be highly symbolic. Art historian James Farmer of Virginia Commonwealth University points out that spirals have symbolized various things to Pueblo Indians—water, migration, the center of the universe—most of which are considered female in nature. The daggers, conversely, are male symbols.

Fertility, then, seems the most obvious symbolic interpretation of the daggers and spirals. This stands to reason, since the purpose of the calendar was to govern agricultural practices and ceremonies. Farmer extends this symbolism to other parts of Anasazi culture—the sunlight penetrating the kiva, the punching of holes in baskets, the coiling fibers in a spiral, prayer sticks called *pahos* stuck into the earth.

Spiral Symbolism

In addition, however, the two spirals go in opposite directions, a common Anasazi and Pueblo design thought to symbolize positive life force in balance with the negative. "Thus," Farmer writes, "the image of a sun dagger penetrating a spiral can be understood . . . as an abstract model of essential, dual, opposing yet unifying universal forces."[19] In what may be a modern version of this concept, Pueblo Indian dancers often emerge from a kiva, move around a village in a set pattern, then, when the dance is completed, retrace the pattern in the opposite direction.

The kiva was then, as now, the center of religious activity. Some nonreligious activity took place there as well. Chaco men, for instance, set up weaving looms in kivas, something their Hopi descendants still do. More rarely, pottery was also formed there. Most artifacts found in kivas, however, are ceremonial, such as nonutilitarian pottery, feathers, fetishes, and *pahos*.

Fragments of wood have survived that may have been part of *tablitas*, the ornate wooden headdresses still used in Pueblo dances. So have remnants of clay pipes that may have been used in much the same way that modern "cloud blowers" are smoked to invoke rain clouds. In general, though, archaeologists have found few artifacts in kivas—logical enough, since sacred objects would not likely have been left behind when the cities were abandoned.

Even though a good number of ceremonial items have been found, virtually no details are known about the ceremonies themselves. Most experts think, however, that they were probably much the same as those of the modern Pueblo Indians, keyed to points on the yearly calendar that had significance for farmers and hunters.

Hopi Ceremonies

In modern times the ceremonies conducted through the year vary from tribe to tribe, but those of the Hopi are typical. In fact, members of other Pueblo tribes consider the Hopi ceremonies the most genuine and the Hopi themselves to be the people most closely in tune with the spirit world.

A Hopi dancer performs during a multitribal gathering in Grand Canyon National Park. Hopi social dances are open to the public, but religious dances are not.

The Hopi year begins in mid-November with *Wuwuchim*, which celebrates the germination of life. The eight-day ceremony begins with the kindling of a fire symbolizing the creation. This New Fire ceremony is one of the few with a direct link to the Anasazi, since similar rites are thought to have been performed in Fire Temple in Mesa Verde. This building seems to have been arranged to allow spectators to surround a large, circular fire pit. Paintings on the wall included zigzag lines and triangles—possibly male and female symbols—and a figure much like Kokopelli, the humpbacked flute player who has been a Pueblo symbol of fertility for centuries.

Next in the Hopi calendar are *Soyal*, around the winter solstice and representing the first appearance of life after germination, and *Powamu* in February, celebrating the season of growing. A major part of *Powamu* is the appearance of the kachinas, spirits who represent animals, aspects of nature, or basic life forces. While kachinas are a major aspect of modern Pueblo ceremonies, there is no indication that they were part of Anasazi ritual. Rather, kachinas are thought to have developed from ancestral contact with the Mogollon people to the south after the Anasazi cities were abandoned.

Various dances throughout the spring and summer implore the gods for rain, and the year ends with three ceremonies—*Lakon, Marawu,* and *Owaqlt*—conducted by women's societies in September and October. Full of sexual symbolism, the first two signify that the crops are coming to maturity and the third that harvest time has come.

The Role of Women

The role women play in Hopi religion is, indeed, very important, although only men are normally allowed to enter the sacred kivas. There are indications that the same was true among the Anasazi. After about 1050, however, priestly class burials included more women, sometimes outnumbering the men.

This elevation of the status of women among the Anasazi may signal the development of the matriarchal clan. The fact that today's Pueblo clans are usually headed by the senior woman and that children automatically become members of their mothers' clans supports this conclusion. After a marriage, the husband moves in with his wife's family, and she is the owner of all property.

With the completion of the women's ceremonies the annual ceremonial cycle is ended. Then, in November, it begins anew. The late anthropologist Frank Waters, an authority on Pueblo religion, acknowledged that the Hopi ceremonies

stem back . . . to the earliest cliff dwellers. . . . Their specific functions are to heal, bring rain, fertilize crops, recount myths, preach sermons, afford fiestas, perpetuate tradition. But above all they are structures to maintain the harmony of the universe. Everything else is partial. Hence their ultimate meanings are rooted in the same old, familiar premise that the unplumbed universe within individual man is indivisibly linked with the immeasurable universe.[20]

The Cannibalism Issue

The long-standing picture of the Anasazi as practicing a peaceful religion centered on nature faced a profound challenge beginning in the 1990s with suggestions that they might have practiced ritual cannibalism. The chief proponent of the theory, Arizona State University anthropology professor Christy Turner, has been studying remains at burial sites for thirty years and believes he has evidence that almost three hundred people were cannibalized at thirty-eight sites throughout the Four Corners.

In a 1999 book titled *Man Corn* (from an Aztec word for a sacred meal of human flesh), Turner and his late wife Jacqueline said the bones they studied showed various signs of cannibalism. Included were cut marks perhaps made when flesh was scraped off, signs of burning, and signs of polishing perhaps made when stirred in a pot.

Turner's thesis is that what he calls a "band of thugs"[21]—Mexican Toltecs among whom cannibalism has been documented—came to Four Corners and used cannibalism to establish control. If true, this might account for the dramatic surge in construction that in some details mirrors buildings in Mexico. It might also account for the appearance of a priestly class.

The Turners' book created a furor in scientific circles and a strong negative reaction among Pueblo Indian leaders, who were outraged at the suggestion that their ancestors could have been cannibals. Such practices, they say, have been confined to witches, outcasts of society.

Some of Turner's colleagues proposed other explanations for the marks on the bones. Archaeologist J. Andrew Darling thinks the marks could have been made when people thought to be witches were executed and dismembered so as to completely destroy them. Debra Martin of

RETICENCE ON RELIGION

Anthropologists think that the Anasazi religion was probably much like that of today's Pueblo Indian tribes. Their comparison is complicated by two factors. First, the Anasazi did not have a written language and left no description of their rituals. Second, the modern Pueblo are often very reluctant to discuss the inner workings of their religion with outsiders.

Most of the knowledge of the Hopi religion, for instance, comes from research done in the first part of the 1900s. As word spread about the elaborate kachina dances, especially one in which dancers hold live snakes in their mouths, serious anthropologists were joined by throngs of tourists, some of whom disrupted the ceremonies in their efforts to take pictures. As a result, very few Hopi dances are open to visitors, and those only by invitation.

The famous photographer of American Indians, Edward Sheriff Curtis, was quoted in Thomas Mails's *Pueblo Children of the Earth Mother* on this reluctance to share their religion:

> Most Indians are loath to reveal their religious beliefs, to be sure, yet with tact, patience, and tenacity the student can usually obtain desired information. On the Rio Grande, however, one meets organized opposition to divulging of information so strong that at Santo Domingo, most refractory of the pueblos, proclamations have been issued against affording information to any white people and at more than one pueblo priestly avengers have in the past executed members who have had the temerity to disregard tribal edicts.

AN OPINION ON CANNIBALISM

The most vigorous scientific debate on the Anasazi in recent years has been cannibalism. Did they practice it? If so, why, and how widespread was it?

Most of the impetus for the discussion has come from the work of Arizona State University professor Christy Turner, whose 1999 book *Man Corn* suggested that Chaco society might have been dominated by a group of people who terrorized the others through cannibalism.

In his Internet article "Sipapu—the Anasazi Emergence into the Cyber World," John Kantner of the Georgia State University anthropology faculty writes that, while the evidence is great that some cannibalism did occur, more investigation needs to be done:

> Some skeptical scholars have stated that the only sure evidence of cannibalism would be the presence of human bone or other residues in coprolites (prehistoric fecal matter). There is no evidence of bone yet, but a recent analysis did identify human myoglobin in preserved human fecal matter from a 12th-century site in southwestern Colorado. . . . Although some detractors have challenged these results as only preliminary and untested, the evidence is quite compelling FOR THAT PARTICULAR CASE. Until these myoglobin results are confirmed with additional testing and other sites exhibit similar evidence, the jury is still out on the frequency of cannibalism in the prehistoric Southwest and the debate continues.

Hampshire College in Massachusetts has studied the bones and thinks that, in addition to executions, the marks could have been caused by wild animals or made in the process of being reburied. "You can't force the evidence to fit a theory," [22] she said.

No Apologies
Turner has remained steadfast in his opinion. "We've said, 'Let's open our eyes and look at the darker side of ourselves,'" he said. "We choose to see it as a group of people coming in and taking over in a very gang-like behavior. [Cannibalism] was their gimmick. This was their weapon. . . . It's not trying in any way to cast any aspersions. It's simply trying to look at it objectively and obtain what the reality was." [23]

Turner's basic premise that cannibalism existed among the Anasazi was bolstered in 2000 with the analysis of human coprolite—dried feces—found in an abandoned Anasazi site in Colorado. Turner's critics had claimed that just because bodies were mutilated, burned, and perhaps cooked did not prove they were eaten. The coprolite, however, showed traces of a protein found only in humans. Considering all the evidence, Doug Owsley of the National Museum of Natural History says, "If it's not cannibalism, I don't know how you'd explain it."[24]

The debate shows little signs of slowing down, but scientists on both sides echo Turner's Arizona State colleague Ben Nelson, who said, "Southwestern archaeology would be poorer without this discussion."[25] Even so, many cannot help but be saddened by this possible stain on the Anasazi. "We would like to believe that all the nasty stuff was introduced by the Europeans, and before that it was all truth, beauty and love,"

said David Wilcox of the Museum of Northern Arizona. "Sorry, that's just not so. These were complex societies. We are all capable of doing those things."[26]

The problem with the cannibalism issue, as with all attempts to reveal aspects of Anasazi religion, is the scarcity of evidence. There are no hieroglyphics to be translated as in ancient Egypt. The petroglyphs and pictographs carved or painted in caves or on cliff faces only add to the mystery. Scientists can agree only that, whatever it involved, Anasazi religion was the core of their lifestyle, much as Walter Hough described the Hopi when he wrote, "If we could pick the threads of religion from the warp and woof [fabric] of Hopi life there apparently would not be much left."[27]

CHAPTER SIX

EVERYDAY LIFE

While the Anasazi made enormous strides in architecture as they advanced from the Basketmaker through the Classic Pueblo periods, their way of life continued the slow pace of change that had marked life in the Four Corners for millennia. Whether living in pithouses or great houses, the Anasazi led a very simple, basic lifestyle. Their concerns were the same as for any people anywhere—obtaining food and preparing it, making a home more comfortable, making clothes and adornments, rearing children, finding time to relax.

In appearance, the Anasazi were probably much like the Pueblo Indians of today. They were shorter than their descendants, probably because their diets were not as generous as they have become more recently. The men averaged about five feet, four inches and the women about five feet. They had a stocky, muscular build, light brown skin, and very little body hair. Their skulls were long and narrow, with high cheekbones.

The Anasazi men wore their jet-black hair long and usually parted in the middle. Many men bobbed their hair by binding the bottom of a tress—one on each side and one in the back—with string and clay. In addition to bobs, some men wore queues, a slender lock of hair, braided or wrapped with string, hanging from the back of the head.

Women's hairstyles changed over the centuries, but less because of fashion than necessity. Earlier Anasazi women cut their hair—probably hacking it off with stone knives—to a length of only two to three inches. They carefully saved the shorn hair, using it to make string and rope. In later centuries, when other cordage material was available, women's hairstyles grew more elaborate, some approaching the modern "butterfly" style of Hopi women with the hair on each side of the head fashioned into large whorls.

Little Clothing

Because of the highly perishable nature of clothing, little remains of the garments the Anasazi wore. Indications are that they wore almost nothing at all in the early centuries, at least in the summer and in warmer climates. Basketmaker women may have worn short aprons and the men loincloths, but so few traces of such garments have been discovered that many experts think that, most of the time, people wore nothing but sandals. Both sexes, though, probably wore some sort of belt, perhaps plaited from yucca fibers, from which to hang tools or other implements needed in the course of a normal workday.

Winter, however, was another matter, and so was life in the higher elevations. Researchers have found remnants of garments—shirts, tunics, leggings—made of deerskin sewn together with rawhide strips or string. The Anasazi also wore deerskin robes and cloaks.

The process of tanning deer hides, if anything like that documented among the Anasazi's modern descendants in the 1800s, was long and delicate. It probably started by soaking the skin in wet ground until the hair loosened and then painstakingly scraping it with a deer rib to remove both the hair and the thin layer of skin just underneath. The hide needed to be

This drawing shows how Anasazi women carried water in large ollas. Water has always been a precious commodity in Anasazi lands, where rainfall is scarce and droughts are frequent.

sponged constantly with water during the process or it would dry out and be ruined.

Once stripped of hair, the hide was left overnight in a solution of boiled animal brains and spinal cords, which yielded the tannin that softened and bleached the leather. Then, after being carefully pulled and stretched until dry, the hide was smoked over a small coal fire to impart a glowing tan color.

Deerskins, however, were not nearly warm enough for use in winter, especially at the eight-thousand-foot altitudes of places like Mesa Verde. For warmth, the Anasazi wore cloaks, lighter ones made from turkey feathers and heavy-duty varieties from rabbit fur. The method for both was the same. The feathers or pelts would be wound in spirals around yucca cords, then sewed together in parallel rows.

Sometimes alternating strips of feathers and fur were used, either to make a medium-weight cloak or simply because the combination was beautiful. The cloaks served as both robes or blankets and, since they were also used as burial shrouds, were evidently highly prized possessions needed in the afterlife.

Weaving Sandals

The one article of clothing worn year-round by everyone were sandals. Like many aspects of Anasazi culture, they grew more elaborate as time went on. Earlier sandals were made by weaving yucca leaves to make a sole or by twisting yucca fibers. These soles were flat, usually square at the toe and rounded at the heel. They were held to the feet by loops of string around the ankles and hooked over the toes. There even seems to have been a form of rain shoes, large sandals of very coarse fibers, examples of which have been found covered with mud.

Later sandals were made out of either plaited yucca or tightly woven string. Many were highly decorated on the upper surface with painted or woven geometric patterns. The bottom of the sole was decorated, too, but with knots and raised strands that formed patterns.

These later Anasazi sandals pose several questions. Why put the design on the top of the sole where it would be covered by the foot and thus not be visible? Why put a raised design on the bottom of the sole where it would quickly be worn off? Thomas Mails suggests that it is "entirely possible that religious and status connotations were involved." The sandals, he writes, just might be about the only piece of clothing a person owned and thus was "their only opportunity for personal expression."[28] As for the raised patterns on the bottom of the soles, they might have been there to provide traction, especially useful when climbing up and down the cliffs.

The Use of Cotton

As time went on, outerwear also became more elaborate, especially with the introduction of cotton and the development of weaving. By the time of the Classic Pueblo period, the Anasazi—usually the men—were weaving cotton cloth for use in both blankets and clothing. They were fond of patterns and achieved them both by painting the finished cloth or using colored yarn. They also used cotton yarn to weave sashes, which previously had been made of plaited dog fur.

While the Anasazi seemingly kept clothing to a minimum, the same was not true of

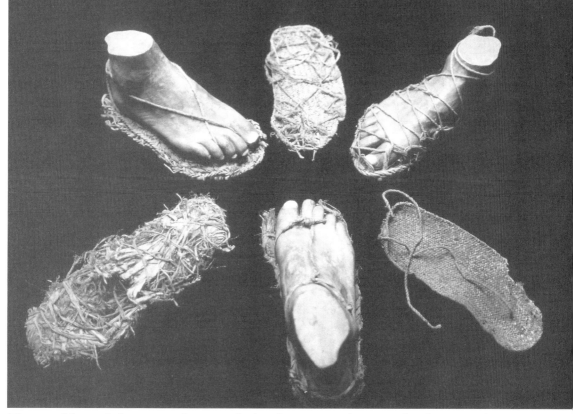

These sandals, made from yucca plants, are displayed at Mesa Verde National Park. During the warmest times of the year, sandals may have been the only item of clothing the Anasazi wore.

jewelry. From the earliest Basketmakers to modern times, they and their descendants have demonstrated a fondness for ornamentation. Most earlier jewelry consisted of beads made from whatever material was handy—stone, bone, or even seeds. They were strung into bracelets and necklaces, often consisting of several strands. Sometimes even animal or bird claws were used for necklaces.

As trade with other peoples grew, the Anasazi were able to acquire other materials. The most popular were shells, particularly abalone, although many others have been found. The jewelry makers most often made the shells into beads but sometimes strung entire shells to form a necklace. Such pieces, because of the value of shells, likely were worn by priests or other persons of high status. Turquoise did not make an ap-

pearance until late Basketmaker times but then overtook shells in popularity. Copper and silver ornaments were rare and acquired only through trade.

Popularity of Feathers

Feathers, too, were popular forms of ornamentation. Archaeologists know from the many bones found that the Anasazi raised turkeys, but they think it was for their feathers instead of their meat. Wild bird feathers were used as well, with those of eagles being especially prized, much as they still are. Parrot feathers, particularly the red and blue of the macaw, have been found in large numbers, although these birds were not native to the Four Corners. Traders from Mexico supplied these, bringing not only macaw feathers but also live birds, skeletons of which have been found.

LIVING QUARTERS

It sounds impressive to say that Anasazi great houses had so many hundreds of rooms, and, indeed, these structures are magnificent for their time and place. "Room," however is a relative term, and it would be a mistake to think of Anasazi rooms in terms of rooms in a modern apartment building. This description of Anasazi living quarters is found in *A.D. 1250* by Lawrence W. Cheek:

> By modern standards, Anasazi living quarters were dark and small. A typical pueblo room might be eight by 10 feet with a ceiling less than seven feet high. There were usually no windows, just a doorway so low that one would have to stoop to enter. Again, it is hazardous to contemplate Anasazi architecture through the lenses of European cultural conditioning. To the Anasazi, "indoors" was for food processing, storage, sleeping, occasionally for cooking, and a refuge during bad weather. Their "living room" was the outdoors.

Feathers were prized for their beauty but probably had religious significance as well. Archaeologists have found bundles of feathers attached to wooden handles. Although they might resemble a modern feather duster, they would hardly have been used as such in the Four Corners and probably were reserved for ceremonies. Experts think this is likely, since many modern Pueblo consider birds to be intermediaries between people and spirits and therefore sacred.

While the Anasazi's bodies might have been adorned, their homes were not. Even though pueblos became larger and more complex, the features of a typical household remained much the same. Shallow fire pits were dug into the floors and lined with stone, although hearths were sometimes built into walls. There was no kind of shelving, and pots were stored either on stone rings or in shallow depressions. Since the Anasazi had no shelves or tables on which pottery sat, the pottery featured round, rather than flat, bottoms.

What storage existed was in the form of niches high in the walls. Although corn was ground in the living quarters—or outside in good weather—it was stored in adjacent rooms built specifically for that purpose. In some of the Chaco great houses, many storage rooms had no connection with living quarters, leading to the suggestion that the grain stored there was for redistribution.

Weaving and Basketry

While most day-to-day activities were done in and around living quarters, at least one craft, weaving, might have been practiced in kivas, places normally associated with religious ceremonies. Remnants of looms have been found in kivas, and, if modern practice is any guide, men gathered there to weave and perhaps use the kiva as a sort of clubhouse. J. Richard Ambler of Northern Arizona University suggests that, if the Anasazi men lived with their wives' families, as is done in some present-day tribes, they might have simply wanted some place in which to come together—without their wives.

While men made cloth, other weaving, such as that of baskets, was done by women. Even after the advent of pottery, there were some purposes for which baskets were more suited, such as to carry loads for which pots would be too large and heavy.

All early Anasazi baskets were made by coiling, a technique that has continued to the present day. This method involves winding willow rods or bundled fibers into a spiral, tightly sewing the resulting coil together, and then shaping it with flat strips, or splints, that would be passed over one layer and under the next. Alternating splints of different colors also provided decoration.

The ring basket appeared later and consisted of yucca leaves plaited together into a mat, which was then curved to make a shallow basin. The ring baskets appear to have been almost strictly utilitarian, with little decoration. Such baskets are still being made and are called "sifters," since they are used to sift grain. The third type of Anasazi basket was wicker, made by interlocking twigs of sumac or rabbit brush. Basketry almost disappeared in the nineteenth and twentieth centuries when cheap containers from other parts of the United States became available, but survived as an art form and now flourishes among many Pueblo tribes.

Rope and string were other aspects of weaving and were highly important, since

The Chacomy style of pottery shows both Anasazi and Mogollon influences. Some modern Pueblo pottery follows the same style.

cordage was used to hold together everything from clothing to weapons. Hair—either human or canine—made the best string, while fibers from a plant known as hemp was a favorite material for rope.

Pottery

Just as important as weaving was pottery, the craft for which the Anasazi have been best known ever since their own time. Pots were made in a bewildering array of patterns and designs, and new styles are being constantly discovered as new sites are excavated. As Ambler writes, "It would be easy, indeed, to spend a lifetime studying Anasazi pottery."[29]

The Anasazi made pottery the same way as most baskets—by coiling. There were, however, a number of steps that had to be done before the pot was formed.

ANASAZI CHILDREN

Little is known about the details of family life among the Anasazi. It is presumed that they were very fond of their children from the way children's bodies were buried, frequently wrapped in a rabbit-skin blanket along with their cradleboard. Infants' bodies have been found buried alongside those of adult females, presumably their mothers.

As with many aspects of Anasazi life, the only comparison is with modern Pueblo people. This description of how Hopi children lived in the early 1900s is from *Dancing in the Paths of the Ancestors* by Thomas E. Mails:

Little boys scarcely able to walk had tiny bows and arrows pressed into their hands, and were encouraged to shoot at brush targets by adults, who applauded heartily whenever they knocked one over. It was common to see several little armed "warriors" on the rooftops guarding the pueblo. Girls played house with the aid of a few stones and considerable imagination. When rain fell and filled the water holes, the children dived immediately into these, splashing around and immensely enjoying the rare treat. Wherever the adults went, the children followed along, searching for the seeds of wild plants or for berries, gathering grass and yucca for baskets, watching the cornfields, gathering the crops, and always having some small share in the work. When a house was being built, they worked almost as hard as their elders, carrying in their little baskets loads of earth or stones with an earnestness that could only be admired.

First, the potter had to find the right kind of clay, remove any impurities, moisten it to the right consistency, and add temper, which could be sand or finely ground pottery, to keep the pot from cracking when fired. After the pot was formed by coiling, the coils were normally smoothed. If decoration was wanted, a thin layer of fine clay called a slip would be applied, polished, and painted. The firing process consisted of covering the pot with wood and setting the wood on fire. It took the right kind of wood burning at just the right temperature to yield the best result. The Anasazi probably first tried to use clay vessels that had simply dried in the sun, only to discover that they cracked too easily when heated. Whether they then developed an effective firing process on their own or adopted one used by neighboring peoples, perfecting this process took many generations.

Community Work

Pottery, like corn grinding and weaving, was often a communal process and perhaps an integral part of daily living rather than put in a separate category of "work." As Charles Amsden writes of modern Pueblo, "They weave them [routine domestic tasks] into their daily lives so smoothly that no word exists to convey the idea that they may be separated from the whole pattern of living."[30]

Since everyone worked, children accompanied their parents everywhere. Mothers strapped their babies to cradleboards slung on their backs. If the mother's work was in one location, such as in a field, the cradleboards might be hung from a tree, where the breeze would rock the babies to sleep.

When they were older, boys probably went with their fathers and girls with their mothers to learn the various skills that would be expected of them as adults. The other part of their education would have been at night, or inside during the coldest days, sitting near a fire and learning from their elders about spirits, gods, and the traditions of their people.

When working, however, both children and parents would have used a very limited variety of tools, all fashioned out of materials at hand. Metal tools were completely unknown in North America until the coming of the Europeans in the 1500s. Instead, the Anasazi shaped wood, bone, and stone into what they needed. Hoes could be made from mountain sheep horns or even thin slabs of stone lashed onto wooden poles with rawhide. Other tools took far more care to construct. For example, awls for sewing had to be laboriously shaped from bone, a process estimated to take at least two weeks.

The Anasazi displayed considerable ingenuity in using resources at hand to manufacture tools. Such ingenuity was extended to other aspects of farming, particularly irrigation. The Chaco Canyon farmers were particularly adept at catching every drop of water and putting it to use. Using a series of dams, they channeled runoff from the canyon rim into a series of ditches. At the ends of the ditches were wooden gates that could be opened to direct water to specific fields or into reservoirs for storage. And with no natural trees or brush to act as a windbreak, they probably built temporary screens to protect young corn plants from the fierce southwestern winds.

Diet and Food Preparation

The corn they harvested was the staple of the Anasazi diet. Analysis of human coprolite from late in the Classic Pueblo period at Mesa Verde shows that corn made up as much as 85 percent of the typical diet. Indeed, one of the most common of all Anasazi tools is the stone metate used to grind corn. Metates of different textures have been found side by side, indicating that corn was ground, perhaps progressively, into meal of varying fineness.

This method of grinding corn had one serious drawback. The action of mano on metate produced a pulverized stone grit that became part of the meal and thus part of whatever was made from it. Over a lifetime, such fare took its toll. The teeth of older Anasazi—although few reached the age of fifty—were often worn down to stubs.

Food preparation was basic and simple. The first step, of course, was to build a fire, which the Anasazi did by the ancient method of rotating a stick rapidly between the hands and using the friction of its point against another piece of wood to kindle a blaze. The process must have been laborious. Scientists have found no evidence that bowstrings or any other devices were used to twirl the fire sticks to make fire-starting easier.

Once the fire was burning, Anasazi women roasted seeds by putting them in a shallow basket along with hot coals and shaking the basket back and forth. Then, after the coals were removed, the seeds were tossed into the air to separate them from the ashes. Meat could be cooked over an open fire or, especially after the development of pottery, boiled. Pottery also made it possible for beans to be added to the Anasazi diet. Corn could be roasted over a fire but probably was more often eaten in the form of cakes made of cornmeal. Women cooked the cakes by placing the dough on red-hot stones, a method still used by the Hopi.

Recreation

As hard as the Anasazi's life was, it would be a mistake to think of it as all work and no play. They had ways other than stories and legends to while away the long winter nights. A form of dice was made from sticks or bone. Grooves cut into these dice served the same purpose as pips, or dots, on the modern cubed version. Another form of what are thought to be gaming instruments consists of sets of seven flat clay discs with beads cemented to the top. No one knows how the games might have been played, however.

Scientists have a better notion of what would have been the purpose of a hoop and two wooden balls found at one site. Many southwestern Indian tribes still have games where people try to throw balls or darts through a rolling hoop.

The Anasazi certainly had music, although it was probably used almost exclusively for ceremony rather than recreation. They made a wide variety of flutes, from the earliest that produced only one sound to styles with multiple finger holes capable of producing a range of notes.

Whistles and rattles have also been discovered, but—somewhat unexpectedly—no drums, except for foot drums in kiva floors. Given that drums are a major part of Pueblo Indian dances today, anthropologists are puzzled by this. Possibly drums of skin stretched over wood frames were developed later or borrowed from other peoples.

LIFE IN THE WINTER

While the Anasazi stayed outdoors as much as possible, winters could be severe in the Four Corners, forcing people inside except when it became necessary to emerge to hunt for food or firewood. In *Anasazi: Ancient People of the Rock*, Donald G. Pike describes what life during the winter must have been like:

> The arrival of winter with the December snows spelled the end of days filled with long hours of work, but it was not a time anticipated with any glee. The cliff dwellings were cold and dank during the winter, usually warmed for only a few hours by the sun, and colds and arthritic pain were constant companions of many in the village. The cold struck hardest at the women and children, because they spent their nights huddled in rooms without fires and their days crouched around fires on the rooftops. In the tiny, poorly ventilated rooms, fires were out of the question for all but the most desperate, they paid for the warmth by choking on the smoke. The men, on the other hand, spent most of their time in the kivas, even sleeping there. Because of the ventilator system [in the kivas], fires could be kept burning in the snug subterranean nests, so the men spent most of the winter out of the cold wind and close by a warming fire.

Very slowly, over thousands of years, the Anasazi had built their civilization in the Four Corners region. They had progressed from rude shelters to multistory pueblos. They had developed sophisticated agricultural techniques, a complex religion, a settled, prosperous way of life. Then, with breathtaking speed, they abandoned what they had built, leaving it to fall quietly into ruin.

CHAPTER SEVEN

ABANDONMENT

What caused the abandonment of the Anasazi great houses? Were the residents pushed—driven off by enemies or epidemics? Were they pulled—attracted by other, more appealing localities? Was it a combination of the two? These are the enduring questions that have confronted everyone who has studied the Anasazi.

From radiocarbon-dating the scraps of wood they have found in the ruins, scientists know that Anasazi builders in Chaco Canyon completed the final additions to the Chetro Ketl great house in 1116. It contained more than five hundred rooms and had required an estimated five thousand trees. Ten years later, it was deserted. Betatakin and Keet Seel at Kayenta and mighty Cliff Palace at Mesa Verde were built, occupied, and abandoned in a period of only fifty years. There are many theories as to why the Anasazi departed that, singly or in combination, are plausible enough. What they fail to explain, however, is why the Anasazi abandonment was so quick, complete, and permanent.

In the decades after scientists began studying the Anasazi, the answer seemed simple and obvious—drought. Water—or lack of if—has been a problem for residents of the Southwest from prehistory to present,

so there was little reason to doubt that the Anasazi, having taken advantage of long periods of favorable climate to build up large communities, were not prepared when rainfall was insufficient to grow enough crops to feed the population.

The Great Drought theory gained strength in the first half of the twentieth century when an examination of tree rings showed that there had, indeed, been periods of severe drought corresponding with the Anasazi abandonment. Chaco Canyon suffered decades of extreme dryness starting in 1090 and again in 1130. In the Mesa Verde area, little or no rain fell from 1276 to 1299.

Conditions, indeed, must have been terrible, and skeletons from these periods show signs that the people suffered from malnutrition and starvation. But as scientists continued to explore the Great Drought theory, they found that it raised more questions than it answered.

Not Much Difference

Droughts, for instance, had long been part of Anasazi life. Other tree ring studies showed that through the centuries there had been even more severe droughts in the Four Corners that had not resulted in wholesale migration from the region. What, researchers ask, was so different about those in the 1100s and 1200s? Why would they result in abandonment of Chaco Canyon, Mesa Verde, and Kayenta, but not other settlements of the times, such as the newly founded villages on the Hopi mesas to the southwest?

Furthermore, were the Great Droughts really all that great? In 1990 a Washington State University graduate student, Carla Van West, startled the archaeological world with her research at Mesa Verde. Calculating from tree-ring data the actual amounts of rain that fell during the drought, she factored in population estimates, soil types, and crop yields. Her conclusion was that there would have been enough food to sustain the Mesa Verde Anasazi. They might

Some Anasazi cites, such as Cliff Palace, were abandoned after only a few decades of occupancy. Drought, enemies, and disease are among the theories to explain why the Anasazi left so abruptly.

THE HOPI LEGEND

Most scientists believe that the Anasazi's abandonment of their Four Corners homeland was not a sudden exodus but instead a gradual drifting away. As conditions in Chaco Canyon, Mesa Verde, or Kayenta began to worsen, a few adventurous people might have set out to find an area where life was better. They might have then acted as a magnet for others, as described in this Hopi legend, found in *Ancient Ancestors of the Southwest* by Gregory Schaaf:

> After some stay [a stranger from the south] left and was accompanied by a party of the Horn [clan], who were to visit the land occupied by their kindred *Hopituh* (Hopi) and return with an account of them; but they never came back. After waiting a long time another band was sent, who returned and said that the first emissaries had found wives and had built houses on the brink of a beautiful canyon, not far from the other *Hopituh* dwellings. After this many of the Horns grew dissatisfied with their cavern home, dissensions arose, they left their home and finally they reached Tusayan [Hopi].

have gone hungry much of the time, but they would have survived. "What her work does is to show that there is not good evidence for a drought so profound that it literally wiped out all farming in the area,"[31] says Dr. William Lipe, who supervised Van West's research.

Furthermore, even if there had not been enough food for all the people, would that necessarily mean that all the people had to leave? The Anasazi had invested considerable time and labor in building the great houses. Would not at least some of them have stayed, despite the lean times? As a point of comparison, modern cities sometimes undergo economic disasters, such as factory closings, that result in many people moving out, but they do not become ghost towns.

Gradual Migration

In fact, some of the Anasazi did stay behind, at least for a while. Recent evidence points toward a more gradual migration away from such centers as Mesa Verde and Chaco Canyon instead of a sudden mass exodus. Still, the question remains: why, when the population had fallen to a sustainable level, did the last Anasazi leave?

And, if the Great Droughts were the cause of the abandonment, why was it permanent? The question is particularly intriguing because as far back as the Archaic period, the Anasazi or their ancestors were known to return to places where they once had lived. The Great Droughts, while long and severe, did not last forever. In a few years, certainly within the living memory of some of the people who abandoned the Classic Pueblo site, the climate moderated. Why did they not go back and take up where they had left off?

Some of them may have intended to do just that. The character of the abandonment was not consistent from place to place. In some cases, indeed, the people took virtually everything with them, even the heavy metates used for grinding corn. Religious objects were removed from the kivas, some of which were then burned. The large amount of broken pottery suggests that some pots may have been ceremonially broken, or "killed." People who left such sites clearly did not expect to return.

At other sites, however, it is as if the inhabitants had gone out, maybe even for a short visit or a walk, expecting to return. Pots were intact, tools were stacked in a corner, and the metates were lined up as always, some of them even containing cornmeal. People in these cities either left in a panic or expected to be back soon.

"There are just too many little discrepancies [in the Great Drought theory]," [32] says Eric Blinman of the Museum of New Mexico. And archaeologist Linda Cordell says flatly, "Nobody is talking about great droughts anymore." [33]

The Impact of Drought
This is not to say that scientists dismiss the severe droughts as irrelevant. After all, says former University of Colorado professor Dave Breternitz, "because the end of the Great Drought period coincided with the abandonment of the general Anasazi area, it continues to be discussed as—if not *the* cause—a contributing factor." [34] And Cordell adds,

> I think [archaeologists] today would comment simply that the Great Drought toward the end of things also coincided with a very dense population for the area . . . in which there were few alternatives. Try living in the area for that long. It's hard to go back to being a hunter and gatherer when you've hunted and gathered everything edible in the vicinity, and your mobility is constrained by the people around you. [35]

Indeed, the strain of trying to grow enough food for a growing population in such arid conditions may have led to what University of California at Los Angeles professor Jared Diamond calls "ecological suicide . . . resulting from inadvertent human impacts on the environment." [36] The Anasazi, he says, might have brought a crisis on themselves by deforestation, cutting all available timber for fuel and construction material. Without timber to help hold it in place, the soil was subject to what geologists call arroyo cutting.

Famine and Disease
Rainfall in the Southwest tends to come in sudden downpours. When runoff forms channels, those channels become deeper over time, finally becoming arroyos, or minicanyons. As arroyos are carved deeper and wider, they not only carry away topsoil, but the water flowing through them is below

the level of the fields. The Anasazi had no system of pumping water up out of the arroyos, so according to this scenario crop yields would have fallen dramatically. The end result, then, might have been social disintegration. "The Anasazi had committed themselves irreversibly to a complex society," Diamond says, "and once that society collapsed, they couldn't rebuild it again because they deforested their environment."[37]

Some scientists think arroyo cutting was a major factor in the abandonment, but others are skeptical. The Anasazi, they contend, had farmed in arid conditions for centuries. They knew the value of water, had developed good irrigation techniques, and would hardly have stood by while their ability to grow food was endangered.

If famine is one possible explanation for the Anasazi abandonment, disease is another. The same population density that strained the agricultural system, inhibited movement, and may have led to deforestation also could have brought about massive health problems. The so-called Great Disease theory was proposed in 1936 by zoologist Harold C. Colton, who thought it possible that, as the Anasazi came together in larger, more populous communities, they became prey to epidemic diseases.

Certainly, conditions in and around the great houses were not sanitary. For centuries, the Anasazi had tossed their trash—and sometimes buried their dead—in heaps next to their dwellings called middens. Such a practice, while certainly not ideal for health, might have not created a severe hazard in small villages or when people moved often. In crowded cliff dwellings, however, it would have been a different story. Urban living was something new for the Anasazi, and the consequences of a lack of sanitation when living in close quarters likely were unknown to them.

While crowding and unsanitary conditions likely caused some disease among the Anasazi, however, there is no evidence of epidemics large enough to have caused people to move away in large numbers. Such epidemics would have necessitated either mass burials or mass cremations, and no signs of either have been found. In addition, there would have been some survivors, and no modern Pueblo legends mention disease as a reason their ancestors migrated to current locations. Indeed, the first known epidemic among the Anasazi or their descendants was smallpox, which was brought by Spanish explorers in the 1500s.

The Warfare Theory

Perhaps, others have suggested, disease was not what caused the Anasazi to flee from their cities, but other Indians. Alfred Kidder, one of the first archaeologists to study the Four Corners, advanced the idea that continual raids by hostile neighbors eventually drove the Anasazi from their homes. Those tribes most frequently mentioned as possibilities include the Utes, Apache, and Navajo, all traditional enemies of the Anasazis' descendants in the post-abandonment periods.

The hostile outsider theory has some problems, however. For one thing, it is not at all certain that some of these tribes were even in the Four Corners at the time of the abandonment. Although the Navajo claim direct descent from the Anasazi, their presence in the area can be documented only as early as about 1300, approximately the same time as the first Apaches arrived and far too late to have an impact on Chaco Canyon. There could have been conflict between these newcomers and the Mesa Verde and Kayenta Anasazi, but it seems doubtful that they would have had the numbers and the mobility—there were no horses—to stage major raids over such a widespread area, although historian Donald Pike points out that raiders, even if they could not successfully attack fortified towns, could loot and even burn Anasazi fields.

Internal Strife

Much more plausible is the idea, suggested by others, including Jonathan Haas of the Field Museum in Chicago, that warfare among the Anasazi themselves might have been a major factor in the abandonment. The idea is that, as population grew and resources shrank, people became much more protective of their territory. Much as a starving man might rob or steal to feed himself and his family, so the Anasazi in an area where crops had failed may have looked with envy toward their more fortunate neighbors. "If you don't have enough food to feed your children, you go raiding," Haas says. "And once I raid you, then you have justification to raid back—the revenge motive. And so warfare becomes endemic in the 13th century."[38]

Clearly, at Mesa Verde both the mesa-top settlements and cliff dwellings seem to have been built with defense in mind. In his work in the Kayenta area, Haas has discov-

Spruce Tree House in Mesa Verde could be reached only from above. Some experts think the Anasazi built their cities in caves to better defend themselves against enemies.

ered "heads without bodies, bodies without heads, extreme defensive site locations, burned villages with bodies lying on the floors."[39]

The Chaco Canyon and Mesa Verde areas, however, show no signs of massive warfare. Besides, opponents of the theory argue, if there had been warfare, the winners would simply have taken over the lands of the losers. The theory, then, still fails to explain why everyone would abandon the area.

A woodcut shows an Anasazi cliff dwelling under attack by members of another tribe. There is little evidence, however, that warfare played a major role in the abandonment of the cities.

While none of the foregoing theories—drought, ecological suicide, disease, and warfare—explain the abandonment, they might well have combined to produce internal dissension—a disquiet profound enough to produce a migration. From all indications, the natural world and supernatural forces were inextricably linked in the Anasazi mind. Living in harmony with oneself, one's neighbors, and the land pleased the gods, who in turn bestowed the blessings of rain and good crops. Dissension, however, threw the harmony off balance, angering the gods.

In the case of Chaco Canyon, at least, the root cause may not have been the drought itself but the interruption of a harmonic pattern. The Chacoan society is thought to have become heavily centered on a religious elite—the priests who controlled the ceremonies invoking divine help and who served as intermediaries between the people and the gods. Rainfall there, while never plentiful, had at least

DISSENSION AND DECLINE

In his discussion of "Why Societies Collapse" on an Australian radio program in 2002, University of California at Los Angeles professor Jared Diamond said that a study of architectural features at Chaco Canyon offers clues as to what might have led to its abandonment:

> When the drought came in 1117, it was a couple of decades before the end. Again any of you who have been to Pueblo Bonito, will have seen that Pueblo Bonito was the six storey skyscraper. Pueblo Bonito was a big, unwalled plaza, until about twenty years before the end, when a high wall went up around the plaza. And when you see a rich place without a wall, you can safely infer that the rich place was on good terms with its poor neighbors, and when you see a wall going up around the rich place, you can infer that there was now trouble with the neighbors. So probably what was happening was that towards the end, in the drought, as the landscape is filled up, the people out on the periphery were no longer satisfied because the people in the religious and political centre were no longer delivering the goods. The prayers to the gods were not bringing rain, there was not all the stuff to redistribute and they began making trouble. And then at the drought of 1117, with no empty land to shift to, construction of Chaco Canyon ceased, Chaco was eventually abandoned.

been predictable, presumably because the priests had properly appealed to the gods.

The Delicate Balance

Starting about 1080, however, some years were much drier than others. The people might have wondered if the balance between them and nature was in jeopardy. Then, in 1090, as David Stuart writes,

Something went horribly wrong. In that year, the traditional prayers must have gone up to the heavens as they had for each of the 90 years before. This time they went unanswered. . . . Nor was there an answer the next year. Nor for four more after that. By the third year, if not the second, the huge storerooms at Chaco lay empty.

LEAVING THE SKY PATH

The idea that the Anasazi abandoned their great houses because they felt abandoned by the gods was employed by modern poet Jeffrey J. Brickley in his 2002 work "Leaving the Sky Path." The following are the final lines of the poem, found on the Web site AuthorsDen:

We have prayed to the Spirits, but They do not answer.

We have dreamed with the Spirits, but we are ignored.

We have walked with the Spirits, but They show us no path.

The Spirits have abandoned us, here on the sky-path.

The Spirits have abandoned us, here in the sky-city.

The Spirits have abandoned us, here in our maize fields.

It is time to wander again the plains and the mountains . . .

It is time to wander again the desert and the forest . . .

It is time to take our children back to the Beginning . . .

Back to the lonely path that our ancestors called home . . .

Until the Spirits find us again, or we all join the Spirits.

We do this not for ourselves, but for our children's children.

We are ageless, we are Anasazi, and we are alone again.

It must have seemed to some Chacoans as if their entire "social con-
tract" had been torn asunder.[40]

According to this theory, it must have
also seemed to the people—and the
priests—that the priests had lost their
power. Somehow, the gods were displeased.
Chaco was the hub of Anasazi society. From
it extended not only roads but also power
and authority. It seems to have been the focus of trade, food distribution, and religion.
When the authority that held it together
faltered, the entire fabric of society began to
unravel.

That social fabric may not have been all
that strong to begin with. For most of their
history, the Anasazi had lived in small
units, most no larger than a village, consisting of an extended family or clan. The coming together of such groups into large
communities, whether for defensive or economic purposes, was very recent and perhaps very tenuous. There was little social
glue binding them together. Anthropologists think, for instance, that different languages may have been spoken even by
residents of the same great house.

A History of Mobility

In addition, the Anasazi had always been
mobile. Their entire history had been one
of migration. Even many of the larger pueblos were occupied only for a generation or
two. As long as rains fell and crops grew, the
people stayed put. But when things began to
go bad, they picked up and moved.

In other words, the Anasazi were not
place-bound in the same way as most modern peoples. It was not as if they were tied to
a location by family history, custom, or sen-

timent. Perhaps leaving the place where
they had been born and perhaps where their
children had been born would not have
been as much of a wrench as it seems to today's city dwellers.

Another factor might have been an entirely different view of land from that held
by modern non-Indians. If the Anasazi were
anything like the modern Pueblo and most
other Native Americans, they did not re-
gard land as something that was theirs,
something to be possessed, but something
from the gods—a sacred gift to be used and
respected. They probably had no concept of
individual land ownership but instead
might have held their lands or houses in a
communal way, perhaps through the clan.
Leaving such an arrangement would be far
different from uprooting oneself from a
homestead in the modern sense.

This is not to imply that abandonment
would have been easy for the Anasazi. Leaving one's home, especially one in which a
family has invested a great deal of labor, is
always difficult, and most people endure
considerable hardship before finally giving
up. Some researchers wonder, then, if the
Anasazi's decision was made easier by something they were going toward in addition to
something they were fleeing from, a combination of forces archaeologists call "push
and pull" factors.

Drought, arroyo cutting, disease, and
warfare are all push factors—circumstances
that would act to drive the Anasazi away.
There are fewer pull factors, but they may
have made the difference.

"Bright Lights"

The simplest pull factor would have been the
one that had governed Anasazi migration for

thousands of years—better living conditions elsewhere. Their ancestors had followed the rains, moving from location to location depending on rainfall amounts. Likewise, if one piece of land became unproductive, they moved to another.

Scientists know that the Anasazi abandonment was not a sudden, impromptu phenomenon but a migration that took place over years, even though most of the movement occurred toward the end. It seems likely that some of the earliest to leave might have maintained contacts with family or friends they had left behind. The distances involved—a few hundred miles—were not so great as to bring about a complete separation. Perhaps, as word of better conditions elsewhere spread among the Anasazi, more and more decided to leave, much as people hunting jobs flocked from rural areas to cities during the Great Depression of the 1930s. Anthropologist William Adams termed this view of the Anasazi migration the "Lure of the Bright Lights."[41]

A much more complex—and more controversial—possible pull factor is that the Anasazi, their traditional religion having proved ineffective in bringing a favorable climate, were lured to a new homeland by a new religion. Throughout the period of the abandonment of the three major Anasazi regions, new settlements were springing up to the south at places like Acoma, Zuni, and the Hopi mesas. A major part of the religion of the people there was—and still is—spirits known as kachinas, from the Hopi *kat-sina*, or "respected spirit."

Kachinas are not gods but spirits—intermediaries to the gods to whom people can pray. They may represent the spirits that Puebloans believe inhabit every object and thus outwardly resemble eagles, turtles, wolves, coal, and stars. They also may represent Puebloan ancestors or the basic forces of life.

The various kachinas are portrayed in colorful ceremonies and dances by members of kachina societies who dress in elaborate costumes and masks. These dances—at least those outsiders are permitted to see—have long attracted throngs of modern tourists. Perhaps, some scholars say, they posed just as strong a fascination to the Anasazi. "There was hot stuff going on down south," says Steve Lekson of the University of Colorado. "There was a new, vibrant, flashy, more democratic ideology."[42]

Welcoming Newcomers

Lending credence to this theory is the fact that the kachina societies, while maintaining secrets, did not limit themselves to members of particular family or clan groups. Instead, they welcomed newcomers to membership. "The ceremonies and beliefs were very successful in integrating Pueblo peoples of different languages and histories," Linda Cordell notes. "They were particularly successful at times of population movement and concomitant [accompanying] social stress."[43]

Other scientists, while they acknowledge the attraction of the kachina societies for other Indian tribes, question whether the cult had established itself in the Southwest in time to provide motivation for the abandonment. Also, they ask, why would the new religion not have simply been adopted in the North rather than causing a mass migration south? Part of the answer may lie in the belief that many Indians have that a place, if the site of disharmony so great as to bring about conflict, may be abandoned by the gods or effectively cursed. This could account for the fact that most of the abandonment took place within a few years and was both complete and permanent. An exciting new religion, combined with a sense that their homeland could never again be productive, might have been the final combination of pull and push.

The Chaco Spirit

The pushes and pulls could have been interrelated over both time and distance, encompassing all the major Anasazi areas for more than two centuries. The full flowering of Anasazi culture was at Chaco Canyon. Nothing, not even the spectacular cliff-dwelling societies of Mesa Verde and Kayenta, came close. Chaco was the heart and soul of Anasazi greatness, its influence felt far beyond even the reach of its road system. When the great beacon of Chacoan civilization went out, the entire Anasazi world must have dimmed. Perhaps the Chaco spirit hung on for another century at Mesa Verde and Kayenta, a reflection of past glory, before it, too, was extinguished.

Scientists generally agree that all the various theories likely worked in combination to produce a spiritual crisis that triggered the abandonment. "You have to look further than the environment," said David

Men representing kachina spirits often wore masks such as this one symbolic of the sun.

Wilcox. "There is a whole social dimension to this process of abandonment that we are only now starting to grapple with."[44]

For whatever reason or reasons, the Anasazi had by 1300 deserted the massive structures that had crowned their centuries of civilization. That civilization, however, did not vanish. It would reappear, much altered but still recognizable, throughout the Southwest, where it endures to the present day.

CHAPTER EIGHT

THE ANASAZI LEGACY

By 1300 the Anasazi had abandoned their ancestral homeland, but where did they go? Virtually all scientists agree that they migrated east, west, and south, combining with one another and with other southwestern peoples to forge a society new in name but ancient in tradition—the Pueblo. As historian Donald G. Pike writes, the Anasazi "are a part of the genetic and mythic memory of men [still] building pueblos of stone, women still shaping their pottery, and young boys learning their way into manhood in the kiva."[45]

The Pueblo themselves certainly do not need scientists to confirm this. To them, the "mystery" of the Anasazi migration is no mystery at all but a fundamental truth handed down through the generations. "You talk to Pueblo people today and they just laugh," says Stephen Lekson of the University of Colorado. "They'll say, 'We'll show you a road map, and show you right where they are; they're us.'"[46]

Although the Anasazi legacy is manifest in the pueblos of Zuni and Acoma, along the Rio Grande, and atop the Hopi mesas, the people dwelling here are not themselves Anasazi in the traditional sense. "I would characterize the period [of abandonment and migration] as a 'reformation,'"[47] says In-

dian pottery expert Toni Laumbach, noting that people from throughout the Southwest were on the move, joining with one another to form new communities with a blend of heritages.

This does not mean that there was no Anasazi influence in these areas prior to the abandonment. Basketmakers lived along the Rio Grande and by A.D. 1100 had begun to make pottery and build pueblos in the same manner as at Chaco Canyon, though not on the same scale or of the same quality. Similarly, the Hopi mesas had long been inhabited by Basketmakers related to the Kayenta Anasazi. Thus, when the abandonment of the Four Corners began, many people likely had some idea of where they were headed.

The Mogollon Migration

At the same time that the Anasazi were moving to the south, the Mogollon were moving to the north from their traditional homelands in southern Arizona and New Mexico. The two cultures met and mingled. "It is impossible today to identify any particular group of the Mogollon with any Anasazi or later Pueblo community," writes art historian Jerry J. Brody. "We can only be sure that, on the one hand, there was an amalgamation of Mogollon and Anasazi people and, on the other, the Anasazi became Pueblo people."[48]

Further west, other changes were taking place. The Hohokam culture virtually disappeared from southwestern Arizona, as did the Sinagua to their north. Scientists think many of these people may have migrated northeast to join the Anasazi on the Hopi mesas; indeed, the modern Hopi count these southerners among their ancestors.

The extent of any integration between the Anasazi and the Navajo, however, is much less certain. Many Navajo consider themselves descendants of both the Anasazi and the earliest Navajo who settled in the Southwest. There is no archaeological evidence of such a connection, and even the Navajo legends are somewhat contradictory. Some place the Navajo in Chaco Canyon at the height of Pueblo III, while others say the land and cities were empty when the first Navajo arrived.

The movements of the Anasazi and other peoples are not clear-cut but rather, as Lekson suggests, "long and convoluted."[49] Most groups probably did not simply move directly from point A to point B but made intermediate stops, sometimes combining with other peoples along the way. Lekson has found traces of Mesa Verde culture as far south as the Rio Alamosa, almost to the

Most experts believe the Anasazi eventually merged with other cultures to form the Pueblo Indians. Pictured here are two members of the Zuni, one of the twenty Pueblo tribes.

Mexican border. Kayenta-style pottery has shown up in the Tucson, Arizona, area, hundreds of miles from the nearest modern Pueblo site. The settlement of such places as Zuni and Hopi thus almost certainly took place over many years, as various groups made their way from their respective points of origin.

The Center Place

Such a migration pattern is, again, no surprise to the modern Pueblo. Hopi legends tell how their communities were built one clan at a time, each one having to prove its ability to provide a needed skill before being accepted. Many Pueblo people have similar legends, telling of years of migration in search of their "center place," a spot designated by the gods to be their homeland.

Edmund Ladd, both an archaeologist and a member of the Zuni, discounts many of the scientific views of the Anasazi abandonment. Speaking at a 1990 conference at the Anasazi Heritage Center in Colorado, he said,

> But *we* [the Pueblo] know why they moved. Because they were looking for the center place. And when they found the center place, that's where

GATHERING OF THE CLANS

Just as most experts think the Anasazi abandonment was a gradual process, they agree that the formation of some of the modern Pueblo tribes was equally protracted. Some groups of Anasazi, having left the Four Corners, might have migrated for generations, joining with others before settling down.

According to Hopi lore, each group coming to the Hopi mesas had to be able to contribute something for the good of all. This account from Andrew Hermaquaftewa of the Bluebird Clan is found in *Ancient Ancestors of the Southwest* by Gregory Schaaf:

> Now when people . . . asked permission to be admitted into the village, the traditional leaders would hold council and consider the question. The newcomers would be asked what could they do by way of helping the Hopi Way of life. The Bluebird Chief must ask them if they have any kind of weapons. All people must leave their weapons of destruction before they would be admitted into the Hopi Village. . . . Boastful people cannot become part of a Hopi Village. Only those who desire to live peacefully, to harm no one, are admitted into the religious order of the village life.

they settled. That's where Zuni is now today. That's where Hopi is. That's where Acoma is. . . . And these are the Anasazi. They moved from the San Juan River basin areas and settled into the modern-day pueblos.[50]

In their efforts to reconstruct the Anasazi migration, scientists look for points of similarity between the abandoned cities and today's Pueblo towns. They examine town plans, architectural features, types of pottery, and petroglyphs and pictographs on cliff faces. They look for similarities in language spoken by the various tribes and clan legends. None of the myriad of clues has furnished a direct, proven link. Linda Cordell notes that while some modern pueblos may have an architectural feature identical to a particular Anasazi ruin, other features will match other Anasazi sites. She says that "there are no known sites that are so closely similar to those of the source areas that they can be considered evidence of a migrant community."[51]

The Language Factor

Adding to the confusion are the similarities and differences between the languages spoken by the modern Pueblo. Each of the twenty Pueblo tribes speaks one of six languages. It would seem logical that speakers of one language, Keresan, for example, would have migrated from the same general area. There are marked cultural differences, however, between the Keresan-speaking Acoma and Laguna tribes, who live only a few miles apart, and especially between these two tribes and the five Keresan-speaking tribes far to the east on the Rio Grande.

Similarly, it would be expected that people from the same clan migrating from the same area would have a common language. Yet all six languages are represented in the twelve tribes that seem to be linked to the Mesa Verde Bear Clan.

There is some resentment among the Pueblo that science cannot accept their traditions as defining exactly who came from where. "One of the things that disturbs me very much . . . is hearing some of these very questions [about where the Anasazi went] continually asked," said Hopi Leigh Jenkins at the 1990 conference. "And not much credence is ever lent, I believe, to some of the ways that Indian people have preserved their history."[52]

Cordell answers that science must deal in "empirical [verifiable] evidence because that's how we are defined and constrained in our scholarship." She adds, however, that "every story of migration that one hears—and that has been collected and recorded among the Pueblos—describes exactly the kind of phenomenon that we would expect . . . of groups separating, of people coming together, of people being all over a landscape."[53]

That, indeed, seems to be what happened, even if the details are sketchy. Group by group, the Anasazi left the Four Corners and gradually coalesced in the areas of the modern pueblos. At first, they constructed pithouses much like those of the Basketmaker days, but before long new cities began taking shape.

Pueblo IV

The first cities of this era, known as Pueblo IV, which lasted until the coming of Europeans in the mid-1500s, tended to

Anasazi architectural features are still seen throughout the Southwest. Pictured is Taos Pueblo of northern New Mexico, perhaps the most striking example of modern Anasazi influence.

be defensive in character. Perched high on mesa tops and in other upland locations, they seem to bolster the notion that the Anasazi were, at least in part, driven out of their homeland. Many of these towns, such as Acoma, Taos, Pecos, and Orabi, are still in existence.

Some of the new cities were huge, larger even than those in the Four Corners. Sapawe, in far northern New Mexico on the Chama River, was the largest known pueblo ever constructed, possibly containing as many as four thousand rooms.

Architecture of the new pueblos was far different from that at Chaco Canyon or Mesa Verde. Easily shaped sandstone was not generally available, so the Pueblo IV people had to build with harder, less workable varieties of stone, which gave the pueblos an irregular, blocky appearance. In some cases, not enough stone of any kind was at hand and the pueblos were built with adobe as in Pueblo I.

The builders did not seem to have any overall design concept as those at Chaco Canyon had. Rather, the large Pueblo IV villages often sprawled haphazardly over several acres. The results were not nearly as graceful or elegant as before, leading some scientists to call the period Regressive Pueblo as opposed to Classic Pueblo. Brody considers the label unfair, pointing out that the Pueblo IV people did not have the same materials with which to work. Besides, he writes, "the differences may only reflect the fact that abandoned stone buildings can be beautiful long after adobe ones have melted back into the earth." [54]

Seasonal Movement

The large, upland pueblos along the Rio Grande were not occupied year-round. They were full in the winter, once the harvest was in and there was plenty of time for social and religious ceremonies. When spring came, however, farmers and their families moved down nearer to the fields along the river or one of the many streams that fed it. Perhaps the Pueblo people eventually felt less threatened from the outside, but they gradually abandoned most of the upland cities and built new ones closer to the river. Many of these communities continue to thrive today.

Although the Rio Grande pueblos were in close proximity to one another—many grouped near present-day Santa Fe, New Mexico—they were never unified to the extent of the Chaco and Mesa Verde cultures. Whereas trade and food distribution had once been conducted on a grand scale, the new pueblos were more self-contained and

THE SCIENTIFIC METHOD

Pueblo Indian people often complain that archaeologists and anthropologists depend too much on scientific investigation and pay too little attention to the oral tradition of the Pueblo. In the book edited by Jerold G. Widdison, *The Anasazi: Why Did They Leave? Where Did They Go?* George Gumerman, professor of anthropology at Southern Illinois University, defends the scientific method:

> We have heard a lot of people [talk] about the value of oral tradition. And I personally feel that archaeologists have not given enough credence to oral tradition. I think some of this has to do with the uncritical acceptance of oral tradition in the late 1800s and early 1900s by archaeologists. My feeling, my honest feeling, is that oral tradition, simply stated such as "this is what we believe," is fine as long as it's considered a statement of belief and not fact. For me it's something that's very important and that should probably be tested and evaluated. I am not asking the people who are talking about their oral tradition to evaluate their oral tradition. For them it's a matter of faith. It's a matter of personal knowledge. But I do, myself, feel that . . . this kind of oral tradition has to be evaluated in a rigorous fashion.

self-sufficient, as if the people wanted to avoid overextending their resources, as might have been the case with the earlier Anasazi. Thus, even today Rio Grande pueblos a half day's walk apart may have different crafts, religious practices, and even languages.

Trade did take place, of course, not only among the pueblos but also with far-distant peoples. The Rio Grande tribes ventured eastward and formed ties with Plains Indians. Rio Grand–style pottery from the period has been found throughout Kansas, Oklahoma, and Texas. Trade routes also went south as far as northern Mexico. Pottery was the primary trading commodity, but the eastern Pueblo also dealt in turquoise, lead for making paint, and clay for making pots.

The Western Pueblos

Trade was much more brisk among the Rio Grande pueblos because of their nearness to one another and the availability of the river as a means of travel. The four western pueblos—Zuni, Acoma, Laguna, and Hopi— were, and still are, much more isolated. This was especially true of Hopi, about 150 miles from Laguna, its nearest neighbor.

Zuni was something of an exception to the rule. It seems to have been the center of a wide trading area, though not nearly on the same scale as Chaco. The multicolored Zuni pottery had a great impact on the development of other Pueblo styles, and they also dealt in textiles, feathers, animal hides, and even excess grain. Some researchers have even suggested that the Zuni language, spoken by no other people and having no relationship to any known language, may have originated as a means for traders to communicate with one another.

Trade was not the only thing that set Zuni apart. As the southernmost Pueblo tribe, it felt most strongly the influence of the Mogollon migration. The kachina cult was very strong, and Zuni may well have been the site where the Anasazi first encountered this new religion. Other customs, such as cremation of the dead, made their first appearances there.

While the kachina cult may have come to the Pueblo via Zuni, it found its greatest expression to the west at Hopi. Unlike most of the other Pueblo tribes, the Hopi have no reliable water supply, no handy river or stream. Instead, they have always relied on dryland farming, which depends entirely on rainfall. As a result, Brody writes, "an intense concern for water and fertility and the ethics of conservation and cooperation seems to have permeated all aspects of Pueblo IV Hopi life."[55] This concern has expressed itself in religious ritual so powerful and elaborate as to have become a model for all other Pueblo tribes. The Hopi are considered by the other Pueblo to be those people perhaps closer than any to the gods, and Hopi symbolism and ceremony have made their way into the rituals of all tribes.

Religion in Art

The Hopi also made religious expression part of their art, and their pottery, its soft, yellow glaze painted with natural and supernatural figures, became popular in the Rio Grande pueblos. Many of the figures painted on the walls of Rio Grande kivas can be traced to the Hopi. It is also the Hopi who are thought to have introduced the "spirit path," a deliberate break in a line surrounding a pot or the inclusion of a tiny line from the interior design of a rug to the

The multicolored pottery of the Zuni greatly influenced the development of other Pueblo styles. This photograph shows a typical polychrome olla made by a Zuni potter.

perimeter. The spirit path, intended to liberate the spirit of the work, remains a feature of both Pueblo and Navajo art.

In the two hundred years after the abandonment of the Four Corners, the Anasazi—now the Pueblo—had built a civilization that rivaled its predecessors in wealth. They had done it, according to David Stuart, by following four precepts: unified communities without elite groups, diversification of the economy, emphasis on conservation of resources, and acknowledgment of the value of efficiency over power. But, just as the Pueblo reached what Stuart called their Golden Age, their world was turned upside down by the most cataclysmic event in the history of the Anasazi or their descendants—the arrival of the Spaniards.

The first Spaniards had arrived in the New World in 1492, but it was not until 1540 that, lured by tales of fabulous cities of gold, an expedition headed by Francisco Vásquez de Coronado made its way to Zuni. Low on food, the newcomers demanded not only that they be given supplies but also that the Zuni acknowledge the authority of Spain. A battle broke out, and Coronado was nearly killed.

As would happen many more times, however, the Pueblo were no match for Spanish armor, weapons, and horses. The Zuni finally got rid of Coronado by telling him that the golden cities lay to the north. He reached the Rio Grande and found no gold, only a string of Pueblo villages, the inhabitants of two of which he proceeded to massacre after they resisted him.

The Spanish Settlement

Coronado's failure to find great riches allowed the Pueblo forty more years of peace before the Spaniards returned. This time they came to stay, bringing with them settlers and Catholic priests. They founded cities such as Santa Fe and Isleta and forced the Pueblo to work the fields for them, whipping or even hanging them if they resisted. The Pueblo religion was banned and kivas destroyed.

The Pueblo, essentially a peaceful people, endured Spanish rule as best they could, but discontent mounted to the point where a full-scale revolt broke out in 1680. In a remarkable feat of coordination among the Pueblo tribes, the rebellion erupted throughout the area on the same day, August 10. In Santa Fe, hundreds of Spaniards were killed, and the survivors, including the governor, had to flee south to present-day El Paso. Even at far-off Hopi, three

SHARING WITH THE SPIRITS

Part of the problem that Pueblo Indians and scientists have understanding one another's viewpoints is the basic concept of the land held by each group. Most scientists come from a European tradition in which the land is something to be occupied, owned, and used. Edmund Ladd, both a scientist and a Zuni, gave the Indian view in *The Anasazi: Why Did They Leave? Where Did They Go?* edited by Jerold G. Widdison:

So many other places are sacred to us because we moved through this country, through this whole country. Our religion is . . . a day-to-day religion. It's every day and every hour of every day that is religious for us. The spirits that occupy the springs, the mountaintops, the four oceans that surround us—all are places where the spirits live, and we share these places with them. And what you [scientists] can't seem to understand is that our world and our universe is limitless. We say, in metaphorical terms, "From the four corners of the world, to the four corners surrounding the world, to the moss-covered mountains and the oceans, the world is our temple." . . . These are not sacred places, but they are respected and venerated places where the spirits live. And we share this land with the spirits. And so when you talk about the Anasazi, think about the people that are living today in the Rio Grande valley, and about the Zuni and the Acomas and the Hopis, because that's what they are.

hundred miles to the west, soldiers and priests were killed and Spanish mission churches burned.

Spain regained control of what was by this time called New Mexico in 1692 when a new governor, Don Diego de Vargas, cleverly managed to break the Pueblo tribes' unity and turn them against one another. Conditions after the reconquest, however, were by no means as harsh as before. The Indians were expected to become Catholics, but most priests turned a blind eye when they practiced their ancient religion in secret.

A People in Decline

The Pueblo did not, however, prosper under Spanish rule. They still were forced to work, with the fruits of their labor going mostly to the Spaniards. Diseases like smallpox and measles, unknown before the coming of the Europeans, took a fearful toll. The Pueblo population, estimated at 69,000 in the 1620s, was down to 6,440 by 1700.

The Anasazi-Pueblo had become, in Brody's words, "a demographically, as well as politically, overwhelmed minority in their own land."[56] This situation grew even more pronounced after New Mexico was granted territorial status by the United States Congress in 1850. Settlers arrived, first in a trickle by wagon, then in a torrent by railroad, and the Pueblo and other Indians found themselves forced onto reservations.

At first, the United States seemed inclined to take up where the early Spaniards had left off. Missionaries tried to stamp out native religions. Well into the twentieth century, Pueblo children were forcibly taken from their parents and put in boarding schools in an effort to "Americanize" them.

Such policies are largely things of the past now. The modern-day Anasazi have their own schools. They practice the old religion freely, although most also identify themselves as Roman Catholics. They have adopted the trappings of modern civilization, and a house more than a thousand years old may sport a satellite dish. Tribal incomes may rely as much on profits from casinos as on sales of traditional crafts.

Modern yet Traditional

These new Anasazi, however, have managed to separate their present and past. They are more than happy to talk by cell phone with their grandson in Albuquerque, but when that grandson visits the pueblo, there are still traditions to be passed along beside a campfire or inside a kiva. After all, their people have been in this land for thousands of years and the white men only a few hundred. Richard Ambler writes that "in view of the tenacity of their culture in the face of past events, it seems likely that the Pueblos have a future as long as their past."[57]

Seasoned by the centuries and toughened by the harsh land, the Anasazi have endured. The kivas of Betatakin are mirrored in those of Taos and Acoma. The melody of the flute played at Chaco Canyon still echoes in Hopi and Zuni. Adobe is made much the same at San Ildefonso as it was at Chaco Canyon. The Anasazi have retained their heritage, one described by Donald Pike as "a lifeway of tradition, strengthened by time and pride, harmonious with the earth and elements, its roots sunk deep in the bedrock of the ancient plateau."[58]

NOTES

Introduction: Empty Grandeur

1. Quoted in Rose Houk, *Cliff Palace*. Mesa Verde National Park, CO: Mesa Verde Museum Association, no date, p. 3.
2. Thomas E. Mails, *The Pueblo Children of the Earth Mother*. New York: Marlowe, 1983, p. 364.
3. Christine Suina, "The Bones of My Ancestors," CNN.com, March 10, 2000. www.cnn.com/2000/NATURE/03/10/america.quest.day5.
4. Quoted in George Johnson, "Social Strife May Have Exiled Ancient Indians," *New York Times*, August 20, 1996, p. C1.

Chapter 1: The Ancient Ones

5. Quoted in Theodore G. Schurr, "Mitochondrial DNA and the Peopling of the New World," *American Scientist* 88, no. 3 (May/June 2000), p. 246.
6. David E. Stuart, *American Anasazi*. Albuquerque: University of New Mexico Press, 2000, p. 15.
7. Stuart, *American Anasazi*, p. 19.
8. Quoted in Tom Higham, "The Method." Radiocarbon WEB-Info. www.c14.dating.com.

Chapter 2: The Basketmakers

9. Quoted in John Kantner, "Sipapu—the Anasazi Emergence into the Cyber World." http://sipapu.gsh.edu/time line.
10. Quoted in Mails, *Pueblo Children of the Earth Mother*, p. 119.
11. Quoted in Mails, *Pueblo Children of the Earth Mother*, p. 94.

Chapter 3: The First Pueblos

12. Quoted in Stuart, *American Anasazi*, p. 57.

Chapter 4: The Great Pueblos

13. Quoted in Mails, *Pueblo Children of the Earth Mother*, p. 214.
14. Quoted in Stuart, *American Anasazi*, p. 77.
15. Quoted in Michal Strutin, *Chaco: A Cultural Legacy*. Tucson, AZ: Western National Parks Association, 1994, p. 19.
16. Linda Cordell, *Anasazi World*. Portland, OR: Graphic Arts, 1985, p. 31.

Chapter 5: Ritual and Religion

17. Mails, *Pueblo Children of the Earth Mother*, p. 201.

18. Mails, *Pueblo Children of the Earth Mother*, p. 172.

19. James Farmer, "Astronomy and Ritual in Chaco Canyon," in *Pueblo Bonito: Center of the Chacoan World*, ed. Jill E. Nietzel. Washington, DC: Smithsonian, 2003, p. 62.

20. Frank Waters, *Masked Gods*. New York: Ballantine, 1950, p. 310.

21. Quoted in Julie Cart, "Did Cannibalism Kill Anasazi Civilization?" *Japan Times*, July 13, 1999.

22. Quoted in Alexandra Witze, "Researchers Divided over Whether Anasazi Were Cannibals," *Dallas Morning News*, June 1, 2001.

23. Quoted in Robert Gehrke, "Anasazi Practiced Cannibalism? One Scientist Thinks So," *Deseret News*, December 30, 1998.

24. Quoted in Gehrke, "Anasazi Practiced Cannibalism?"

25. Quoted in Witze, "Researchers Divided."

26. Quoted in Cart, "Did Cannibalism Kill Anasazi Civilization?"

27. Quoted in Don Talayesva, *Sun Chief: The Autobiography of a Hopi Indian*, ed. Leo Simmons. New Haven, CT: Yale University Press, 1942, p. 17.

Chapter 6: Everyday Life

28. Mails, *Pueblo Children of the Earth Mother*, p. 138.

29. J. Richard Ambler, *The Anasazi: Prehistoric People of the Four Corners Region*. Flagstaff, AZ: Museum of Northern Arizona, 1989, p. 36.

30. Quoted in Mails, *Pueblo Children of the Earth Mother*, p. 115.

Chapter 7: Abandonment

31. Quoted in George Johnson, "The Anasazi 'Collapse,'" *New York Times*, August 20, 1996.

32. Quoted in Johnson, "Anasazi 'Collapse.'"

33. Quoted in Jay W. Sharp, "The Great Puebloan Abandonments and Migrations," DesertUSA. www.desertusa.com/ind1/ind_new/ind12.html.

34. Quoted in Jerold G. Widdison, ed., *The Anasazi: Why Did They Leave? Where Did They Go?* Albuquerque, NM: Southwest Natural and Cultural Heritage Association, 1991, p. 18.

35. Quoted in Widdison, *The Anasazi*, p. 25.

36. Jared Diamond, "Why Societies Collapse: Jared Diamond at Princeton University," Australian Broadasting Company, Background Briefing. www.abc.net.au/rn/talks/bbing/stories/s743310.htm.

37. Diamond, "Why Societies Collapse."

38. Quoted in Johnson, "Anasazi 'Collapse.'"

39. Jonathan Haas, "The Archaeology of War," Iranian Cultural Heritage News Agency (CHN). www.chn.ir/english/showearticle.asp?no=17.

40. Stuart, *American Anasazi*, p. 119.

41. Quoted in Widdison, *The Anasazi*, p. 19.

42. Quoted in Johnson, "Anasazi 'Collapse.'"

43. Quoted in Sharp, "Great Puebloan Abandonments and Migrations."

44. Quoted in Johnson, "Anasazi 'Collapse.'"

Chapter 8: The Anasazi Legacy

45. Donald G. Pike, *Anasazi: Ancient People of the Rock*. Palo Alto, CA: American West, 1974, p. 162.

46. Quoted in Peter N. Spotts, "Vanishing Act," *Christian Science Monitor*, August 31, 2000.

47. Quote in Spotts, "Vanishing Act."

48. Jerry J. Brody, *The Anasazi: Ancient Indian People of the American Southwest*. New York: Rizzoli International,

1990, p. 186.

49. Stephen H. Lekson, "Flight of the Anasazi," *Archaeology* 54, no. 5 (September/October 2001).

50. Quoted in Widdison, *The Anasazi*, p. 35.

51. Quoted in Sharp, "Great Puebloan Abandonments and Migrations."

52. Quoted in Widdison, *The Anasazi*, p. 31.

53. Quoted in Widdison, *The Anasazi*, p. 52.

54. Brody, *The Anasazi*, p. 191.

55. Brody, *The Anasazi*, p. 214.

56. Brody, *The Anasazi*, p. 222.

57. Ambler, *The Anasazi*, p. 4.

58. Pike, *Anasazi*, p. 166.

FOR FURTHER READING

Books

Eleanor H. Ayer, *The Anasazi*. New York: Walker, 1993. Survey of Anasazi culture from the Basketmakers to the modern Pueblo with special attention given to archaeological techniques.

Franklin Folsom, *Indian Uprising on the Rio Grande: The Pueblo Revolt of 1680*. Albuquerque: University of New Mexico Press, 1996. Award-winning account of rebellion is told from the Native American point of view, comparing their motives to that of American colonists in 1776.

Arthur Day Grove, *Coronado's Quest*. Berkeley: University of California Press, 1982. Reprint of the 1940 book on Coronado's explorations. A long yet highly readable book for the serious student.

Frank McNitt, *Richard Wetherill: Anasazi*. Albuquerque: University of New Mexico Press, 1966. Fascinating biography of the Colorado cowboy who discovered and explored many of the most famous Anasazi sites.

Web Sites

Anasazi Heritage Center (www.co.blm.gov/ahc). Wide variety of information disseminated by the Anasazi Heritage Center, a branch of the Colorado Bureau of Land Management.

DesertUSA (www.desertusa.com). Section titled "Desert Peoples and Cultures" has extensive information on the Anasazi as well as other prehistoric peoples of the Southwest and the present-day Pueblo tribes.

Works Consulted

Books

J. Richard Ambler, *The Anasazi: Prehistoric People of the Four Corners Region*. Flagstaff, AZ: Museum of Northern Arizona, 1989. Excellent overview of the Anasazi by a leading anthropologist with beautiful photography by Marc Gaede.

F.A. Barnes and Michaelene Pendleton, *Prehistoric Indians: Their Cultures, Ruins, Artifacts and Rock Art*. Salt Lake City, UT: Wasatch, 1979. Especially good accounts of how ancient artifacts are sought, found, preserved, and collected.

Jerry J. Brody, *The Anasazi: Ancient Indian People of the American Southwest*. New York: Rizzoli International, 1990. Excellently written and illustrated survey of the Anasazi from the perspective of an art historian.

Lawrence W. Cheek, *A.D. 1250: Ancient Peoples of the Southwest*. Phoenix: Arizona Highways, 1994. Good descriptions, not only of Anasazi development but also of each major site.

Linda Cordell, *Anasazi World*. Portland, OR: Graphic Arts, 1985. Highly informative account by one of the Southwest's leading archaeologists. Photographs by Dewitt Jones.

———, *Prehistory of the Southwest*. Orlando, FL: Academic Press, 1984. Scholarly account of the development of the Anasazi and other peoples by one of the field's most respected experts.

Kendrick Frazier, *People of Chaco: A Canyon and Its Culture*. New York: W.W. Norton, 1986. Account of the Chaco Canyon culture and the mysteries surrounding it by a veteran writer on supernatural subjects.

Rose Houk, *Cliff Palace*. Mesa Verde National Park, CO: Mesa Verde Museum Association, no date. Full of both facts about and pictures of Cliff Palace, this pamphlet is sold to visitors in the park.

Harry C. James, *Pages from Hopi History*. Tucson: University of Arizona Press, 1974. One of the best sources available on Hopi history after the arrival of the Spaniards. Especially good section on 1880–1930 interactions with Anglo-Americans.

Thomas E. Mails, *Dancing in the Paths of the Ancestors*. New York: Marlowe, 1983. Very comprehensive account of the lives and cultures of the present-day Pueblo tribes. Companion volume to *The Pueblo Children of the Earth Mother*.

———, *The Pueblo Children of the Earth Mother*. New York: Marlowe, 1983. Richly detailed account of the Anasazi and surrounding peoples, amply illustrated by the author.

Jill E. Nietzel, ed., *Pueblo Bonito: Center of the Chacoan World*. Washington, DC: Smithsonian, 2003. Collection of essays by experts in various fields on different aspects of the Chaco Canyon great house.

David Grant Noble, ed., *Houses Beneath the Rock*. Santa Fe, NM: Ancient City Press, 1986. Collection of six essays on different aspects of the Anasazi of Canyon de Chelly in Arizona.

Donald G. Pike, *Anasazi: Ancient People of the Rock*. Palo Alto, CA: American West, 1974. Highly detailed information on the Anasazi is interspersed with sections of photography by David Muench.

Gregory Schaaf, *Ancient Ancestors of the Southwest*. Portland, OR: Graphic Arts Center, 1996. Superb photography by Lewis Kemper and the inclusion of many traditional Indian stories sets this book apart from others on the same subject.

Michal Strutin, *Chaco: A Cultural Legacy*. Tucson, AZ: Western National Parks Association, 1994. Very informative account of what life was like among the Chaco Anasazi. Color photographs by H.H. Huey.

David E. Stuart, *American Anasazi*. Albuquerque: University of New Mexico Press, 2000. Examines the rise and fall of the Chaco Canyon culture and its implications for the present.

Gene S. Stuart, *America's Ancient Cities*. Washington, DC: National Geographic Society, 1988. Colorfully written and wonderfully photographed book describing ancient cities throughout North America and Mesoamerica.

Don Talayesva, *Sun Chief: The Autobiography of a Hopi Indian*. Edited by Leo Simmons. New Haven, CT: Yale University Press, 1942. Fascinating first-person story of a Hopi born in 1892 and the changes he saw come to his people.

Frank Waters, *Masked Gods*. New York: Ballantine, 1950. Extensive study of rites and ceremonies among the Navajo and Pueblo tribes of the southwestern United States.

Don Watson, *Indians of the Mesa Verde*. Mesa Verde National Park, CO: Mesa Verde Museum Association, 1961. Dated but still useful season-by-season account of prehistoric life at Mesa Verde.

Jerold G. Widdison, ed., *The Anasazi: Why Did They Leave? Where Did They Go?* Albuquerque, NM: Southwest Natural and Cultural Heritage Association, 1991. Verbatim transcription of conference panel discussion by both scientists and Pueblo tribe members.

Periodicals

Jerry Bishop, "Strands of Time," *Wall Street Journal*, September 10, 1993.

Julie Cart, "Did Cannibalism Kill Anasazi Civilization?" *Japan Times*, July 13, 1999.

Robert Gehrke, "Anasazi Practiced Cannibalism? One Scientist Thinks So," *Deseret News*, December 30, 1998.

George Johnson, "The Anasazi 'Collapse,'" *New York Times*, August 20, 1996.

———, "Social Strife May Have Exiled Ancient Indians," *New York Times*, August 20, 1996.

Stephen H. Lekson, "Books: Chaco Death Squads," *Archaeology* 52, no. 3 (May/June 1999).

———, "Flight of the Anasazi," *Archaeology* 54, no. 5 (September/October 2001).

Stephen H. Lekson, Thomas C. Windes, John R. Stein, and W. James Judge, "The Chaco Canyon Community," *Scientific American*, July 1988.

Theodore G. Schurr, "Mitochondrial DNA and the Peopling of the New World," *American Scientist* 88, no. 3 (May/June 2000).

Peter N. Spotts, "Vanishing Act," *Christian Science Monitor*, August 31, 2000.

Alexandra Witze, "Researchers Divided over Whether Anasazi Were Cannibals," *Dallas Morning News*, June 1, 2001.

Internet Sources

Australian Broadcasting Company, "Why Societies Collapse: Jared Diamond at Princeton University," Background Briefing. www. abc.net.au/rn/talks/bbing/stories/s743310.htm.

Jeffrey J. Brickley, "Leaving the Sky Path," AuthorsDen.com. www. authorsden.com/visit/viewpoetry.asp?AuthorID=6675&id=12048.

Daniel Gibson, "When the Earth Cracked: Mysteries of the Anasazi," *Cowboys & Indians Magazine*, July 1997. www.cowboysindians. com/articles/archives/0797/anasazi.html.

Jonathan Haas, "The Archaeology of War," Iranian Cultural Heritage News Agency (CHN). www.chn.ir/english/showearticle.asp?no=17.

Tom Higham, "The Method," Radiocarbon WEB-Info. www.c14dating. com.

John Kantner, "Sipapu—the Anasazi Emergence into the Cyber World." http://sipapu.gsu.edu/timeline.

Jay W. Sharp, "The Great Puebloan Abandonments and Migrations," DesertUSA. www.desertusa.com/ind1/ind_new/ind12.html.

Christine Suina, "The Bones of My Ancestors," CNN.com, March 10, 2000. www.cnn.com/2000/NATURE/03/10/america.quest.day5/.

INDEX

Picture Credits

About the Author

William W. Lace is a native of Fort Worth, Texas, where he is executive assistant to the chancellor at Tarrant County College. He holds a bachelor's degree from Texas Christian University, a master's degree from East Texas State, and a doctorate from the University of North Texas. Prior to joining Tarrant County College he was director of the News Service at the University of Texas at Arlington and a writer and columnist for the *Fort Worth Star-Telegram*. He has written more than twenty-five books for Lucent, one of which—*The Death Camps*—was selected by the New York Public Library for its 1999 Recommended Teenage Reading List. He and his wife, Laura, a retired school librarian, live in Arlington, Texas, and have two children and three grandchildren.